A WORTHWHILE AND MEANINGFUL CAREER IN GLOBAL HEALTH AT THE WORLD BANK

Reviewing HIV/AIDS data in Guyana.

A WORTHWHILE AND MEANINGFUL CAREER IN GLOBAL HEALTH AT THE WORLD BANK

An Autobiography

WILLY DE GEYNDT

SMALL BATCH BOOKS
Amherst, Massachusetts

Printed in the United States of America.

On the cover: The World Bank headquarters, in Washington, D.C.
Photo by By Shiny Things-Flickr, CC BY 2.0,
https://commons.wikimedia.org/w/index.php?curid=2390362

Cover and text design by Mary A. Wirth

SMALL
BATCH
BOOKS

493 SOUTH PLEASANT STREET

AMHERST, MASSACHUSETTS 01002

413.230.3943

SMALLBATCHBOOKS.COM

CONTENTS

INTRODUCTION

Chronicling events where I am the central figure is a daunting experience. Yet it has been enjoyable to revisit and relive the successes and failures of a meaningful career. I dedicate this book to the many colleagues at the World Bank Group and in academia who helped and supported me in my global career.

A WORTHWHILE AND MEANINGFUL CAREER IN GLOBAL HEALTH AT THE WORLD BANK

1 A FORTUITOUS MEETING: 1981

A seminal event that defined my health services career happened in June 1981 as a result of a fortuitous encounter. The first International Course on Education for Health Services Administration was organized in Lisbon June 15 to July 3, 1981, by the National School of Public Health of Portugal in collaboration with the Association of University Programs in Health Administration. AUPHA President Gary Filerman invited me to participate in this event, which was held in the modern Calouste Gulbenkian Museum.

At an evening reception at the Castelo de São Jorge, I noticed an Indian lady wearing a beautiful sari, so I introduced myself. Her name was Ishrat Z. Husain, and she was one of three division chiefs in the newly created Population, Health, and Nutrition (PHN) Department at the World Bank. We had a long and interesting conversation but did not meet again during this event. I had no idea what the career consequences would be as a result of participating in this course and from the happenstance meeting with a World Bank manager.

In August 1981 I received a call from a staff member of Ishrat Husain's division inviting me to a meeting at the World Bank to discuss a potential consultancy assignment. His name was Pepe Andreu. On August 23 I met with Ishrat and Pepe and we agreed on a consultancy to Colombia in September. This monthlong assignment took me first to D.C. on September 23 for a briefing and to collect travel documents and advance travel expenses. On September 26 I flew to Bogotá first to meet with Ministry of Health officials for two days, and then continued to Manizales, capital of the Department of Caldas. Manizales is the main center for the production of Colombian coffee and an important hub for higher educational institutions. To support my analysis of the health system of the Caldas Department, I visited urban and rural healthcare facilities and health workforce educational and training institutions, and interviewed a large number of staff over a two-week period, collecting copious materials. I returned to Bogotá for a one-day debriefing, then flew home on October 23 to type my report in my home office (no computers yet—just typewriters and carbon copies).

The report must have been well received, as I was invited back to Washington, D.C., December 13 to 18, 1981 at which time I met the personnel director of the World Bank, Mr. Cornelis de Kievit.

2 GLOBAL HEALTH CAREER AT THE WORLD BANK: 1982–1997

1982: Brazil, Colombia, Chile

The year started out with my second consultancy for the World Bank, traveling to Rio de Janeiro and São Paulo in Brazil from January 8 to 25, 1982. I returned via the World Bank headquarters, for a one day debriefing with John Evans, the director of the PHN Department, my future division chief, Stephen Denning; and assistant division chief, David Pearce. My third World Bank consultancy took me back to Colombia in March, spending one day in Bogotá, then two days in Cartagena, and then back to Bogotá for one week. I left Colombia to fly to Washington for debriefing and for job interviews with division chiefs Denning and Messenger, K. Kanagaratna (head of the population sector), and David Pearce.

I went to Santiago on May 31 for one week at the invitation of a US consulting company headed by Jim Rice to provide technical assistance to the health maintenance organization Banmédica. What is most memorable about this trip is that I received a phone call from the World Bank informing me that they were offering me a position and asking me to come by to sign the necessary documents. The 10:00 p.m. flight on June 7 arrived at 10:00 a.m. the next morning in Washington. The meeting with the personnel manager, Mr. de Kievit, took place on June 10 at 2:30 p.m., when I formally accepted to become a staff member of the World Bank starting September 1, 1982. We negotiated and agreed on an annual net starting salary of $47,000. This was almost $4,000 a month after taxes. To put this in perspective, fifteen years earlier I had lived with my wife and two children on a $400-a-month scholarship from the W.K. Kellogg Foundation in student housing in Saint Paul, Minnesota.

Moving!

The packers arrived on August 26 at my home in St. Paul, Minnesota, and the movers on August 27. We stayed one night at the home of Charles H. Mayo II and left Minnesota on August 28 being guests for two nights at the Bobenrieth family in Potomac, Maryland. We moved into a rented house in Carderock, Md on Monday, August 30 for one year and purchased a house in Cabin John Md in August 1983.

Drawing upon my experience visiting health care facilities in rural areas and in large metropolitan areas in Latin America and Africa, I published "Urban Versus Rural Primary Health Care in Developing Countries: Similarities and Differences," *Bulletin*, PAHO, 1982.

The Genesis of the Health Sector at the World Bank

The Bank adopted a health policy in 1974 that limited its operations in the health sector to the financing of health components of projects in other sectors. In 1975, a Bank health sector policy paper suggested that poor health conditions were impeding development in many countries and that the improvement of health should be a major development objective. Subsequently, the Bank increased its activities in the health sector. From 1975 through 1978, the Bank provided technical and financial assistance to 44 countries for 70 health components of projects in other sectors - mainly in agriculture - amounting to $405 million. In addition, the Bank prepared seven health sector studies. This marked a significant and rapid increase in a new area of Bank activity. Bernhard Liese from Bonn, Germany joined the Bank in 1976 as a tropical disease specialist and was joined in 1979 by Oscar Echeverri from Cali, Colombia. The World Bank's seminal

"Health Sector Policy Paper" was published in February 1980. Fredrick Golladay was the author and Bernhard Liese and Alexa Dru Deric contributed substantially to the research.

In July 1979, the Executive Directors reviewed the Bank's experience in financing health components and approved a proposal to provide direct lending for health projects in addition to financing health components as in the past. The new Population, Health, and Nutrition (PHN) Department was to start slowly, beginning with one health project in fiscal 1981 and expand to four or five projects annually by 1984. John Evans was the first director of the PHN Department. Kandiah Kanagaratnam - called K.K. - was a pioneer in the population area and the nutrition area benefitted from the dynamic leadership of Alan Berg. Several mid-career public health specialists were recruited, including me, Anthony Measham, Michael Porter, Stan Scheyer, Margaret Saunders, Jacques Baudouy, and Jean-Louis Lamboray. David de Ferranti joined in 1981 as a health economist. Subsequently, this seasoned group of health professionals mentored the incoming younger generation of health specialists such as Xavier Coll and Patricio Marquez. Note that the PHN Department was renamed HNP when Sir Richard Feachem was the Director of the Department in the late 1990's as the size of the health portfolio was by far the largest of the three sectors.

Incidentally, I had met K.K. In 1973 to discuss a project evaluation consultancy in Tunisia. A demographer in the population department, Ferdinand Rath, had come across my research and publications on program evaluation and invited me to join an upcoming mission to Tunisia. I accepted the invitation. However, the date of the mission was postponed to later in the year and conflicted with my fall semester teaching load at the University of Minnesota School of Public Health.

First Year at The World Bank

September 1, 1982, was my first day as a staff member of the International Bank for Reconstruction and Development (IBRD). The appointment at the World Bank assured me a monthly paycheck and generous fringe benefits, including medical insurance coverage, vacation and sick leaves, defined pension benefits, borrowing for my children's college education at low interest rates, upgraded flying class, and comfortable hotels.

The first year was stressful adapting to a new organizational culture with its procedures and rules. First, I found out that the first year of employment was a probation year. This offended me given my vast international experience, linguistic skills, and demonstrated writing skills. Why would I be on probation when I had already proven myself? However, my division chief, Stephen Denning, shortened the probation period and, after nine months, converted it to a permanent position. Second, I was assigned to the only available office in the division, which happened to be a windowless corner office. I was quite upset about this arrangement, remembering my eighth-floor corner office in Brussels overlooking a park and my university and home offices in Minnesota. In addition, this office contained the electric fuse boxes for the floor and an emergency exit door to access the stairwell. Workers would come in occasionally to check the fuse boxes. The office was in an old building called the N building located on the corner of 19th and H Street NW. It was a rental building later demolished and replaced with a modern office building. My office neighbor was Tony Measham, a Canadian physician with wide international experience, also in a windowless office but without fuse boxes! The advantage of an old office building were the large offices and the wide space in the middle—a far cry from today's small offices and cubicles that maximize space. Third, my first internal memo and first external draft communication to a country were returned to me by the division chief with many edits. I was shocked to find out that my writing was not good enough given my record of publications reviewed by professional editors. I had to learn to write Bank-style. My division chief sat down with me and patiently explained and taught me how to write in an acceptable style.

Computers were not common yet and reports were written out longhand on yellow pads and then typed by a secretary. The typed draft was then reviewed, corrected, and sent back to the secretary to make the necessary changes. This process could take many iterations. The division chief managed to obtain a few computers for the division, which were put on a rolling table and shared among staff. We had to put in our claim and wait for our turn to use the computer. WordPerfect may have been the word processor that we used in the early eighties.

The first two months were taken up by orientation meetings, training sessions on how to report project progress, learning disbursement procedures, explanations of personnel benefits, luncheons with colleagues, and in general becoming comfortable in the bureaucratic environment.

My first operational WB assignment was a long four-week mission to São Paulo, Brazil, from November 21 to December 4, followed by ten days in Rio de Janeiro. The São Paulo project included the addition of five hospitals in the sprawling metropolitan area. The project was controversial within the WB: First, questions were raised as to why the WB should provide support to the wealthiest state in Brazil and, second, why finance the construction of hospitals and not support primary health care that is more cost effective as evidenced by economic analysis of return on investment? This was the first health project in Brazil, and it was critical that it be successful and become a model for other states. Why would one start a first-time operation in a poor state unlikely to be successful? As it turned out, local staff trained during project execution were able to provide technical assistance to other states, thus creating a multiplier effect. Primary health care was incorporated in the outpatient departments of the hospitals. When needing medical care, people always go first to a hospital.

The WB provided support to a workshop in Rio organized by WHO/PAHO on the inclusion of strategic management education in health administration courses. I made two presentations in Spanish. The first one was an integrative framework on "Implementation of Policies and Strategies in the Health Sector." The second one presented a framework for the selection of an implementation strategy using a SWOT analysis (strengths, weaknesses, opportunities, and threats) of the internal and external environments. WB staff also attended the workshop.

1983: Egypt, Lebanon, Paraguay, Jordan, Tunisia

The World Bank is organized into six geographic regions: Latin America and the Caribbean (LAC), the Middle East and North Africa (MENA), Africa (AFR), Europe and Central Asia (ECA), South Asia (SAR), and East Asia and the Pacific (EAP). The Population, Health, and Nutrition Department (HNP) was still in its infancy, and each of the three HNP operational divisions covered two geographic regions. In my case, I worked in the division responsible for LAC and MENA, and mission travels in 1983 took me to Egypt, Lebanon, Jordan, Tunisia, and Paraguay.

The two-week mission to Egypt starting January 16 was my second visit to Cairo. I had spent three days sightseeing two years earlier, prior to flying to Saudi Arabia on a consultancy. We first held meetings with the Ministry of Health in Cairo, followed by field visits to hospitals and health clinics in four administrative governorates: Cairo, Qalyubia, Kafr El Sheikh in the lower Delta area, and Giza, home to the Great Sphinx and the Pyramids of Giza. I recall the generous hospitality at the clinics we visited, where we were always welcomed with a large selection of local dishes. A UNFPA representative, Sheila Macrae, participated in this mission. The WB team leader's idea of nurturing team spirit and encouraging teamwork was a negative lesson for me. A team meeting at 6:00 p.m. in his hotel room meant ordering drinks and talking about the mission and other—not always relevant—topics for hours, with dinner not until 9:00 p.m. When I became team leader, I limited team meetings to one hour at 5:30 or 6:00 pm prior to dinner. One hour is sufficient to review the day's activities and team members can then decide where to dine, and with whom (or alone). Usually, it would be a team dinner anyway.

The civil war conflict in Lebanon seemed to have been resolved. The WB shared in the optimism and organized a large reconstruction mission on February 12. Seven economic sectors were included in the twenty-three-person team. The task team leader was Abdallah El Maaroufi. Representing the health sector, I met with the minister of health and his staff, with other international partners (USAID, WHO, UNICEF), and with staff from the School of Public Health of the American University of Beirut (AUB). Data collected allowed me to make an inventory of the financial requirements to restore the health system to its pre-civil war operational capacity. During this trip I met future WB colleagues, Susan Stout, who was in Lebanon as a USAID consultant, and Eva Jarawan, who was an Assistant Professor at the School of Public Health of AUB, who was appointed health specialist at the WB in 1991, joined me on the faculty at Georgetown University starting with the academic year of 2015-16 as Assistant Professor and promoted to Associate Professor in 2022.

The WHO Regional Office for the Eastern Mediterranean

(WHO/EMRO) is located in Alexandria, Egypt, and I was tasked with debriefing the regional director. I flew to Cairo on Saturday, February 26, and took a bus to Alexandria, staying at the Delta Hotel. Alexandria is the second-largest city in Egypt and a major economic center, extending about thirty-two kilometers (twenty miles) along the coast of the Mediterranean Sea. It is a popular tourist destination founded around a small, Ancient Egyptian town, circa 332 BC, by Alexander. On Wednesday, March 2, I took the train back to Cairo, staying one night at the Sheraton Heliopolis before flying to Brussels the next morning and back to Washington, D.C., on Monday, March 7.

In April I visited Paraguay for the first time, one of only two landlocked countries in South America (the other is Bolivia). We left on Sunday, April 10, arriving in Rio de Janeiro on Monday morning, and traveling via Curitiba and Foz do Iguaçu to the capital, Asunción. The detour to Foz do Iguaçu allowed us to visit the spectacular Iguaçu Falls located on the border of Argentina and Brazil and consisting of approximately 257 individual falls over 2.7 kilometers (1.7 miles) chosen as one of the "New Seven Wonders of Nature."

In Paraguay we assessed the health infrastructure of the country and the health status of the population, visiting health facilities and meeting with government officials. I was shocked one day to see in the Asunción newspaper a photo of the U.S. embassy in Beirut damaged by the explosion of a truck at the entrance next to the cafeteria, where two months earlier I had lunched with my USAID colleagues.

I went back to Beirut on Wednesday, June 15, staying only two days to meet with the minister of health twice and have dinner with my friend and colleague Nabil Kronfol. I flew from Beirut to Jordan to join the WB team. We had one week of meetings with the Research and Planning Department of the Jordan Ministry of Health, with one full day spent assessing the functionality of Al-Bashir Hospital, a deteriorating public hospital. Subsequent discussions dealt with what the best way forward would be: to close, to rehabilitate and fix the worst parts, or to replace the hospital. Friday is the weekly Muslim holiday, and I used that time to drive south and visit the famous city of Petra, an archaeological site and Jordan's most visited tourist attraction. Petra is accessed through a gorge, three-quarters of a mile long, called the Siq, which leads directly to the Khazneh temple. Famous for its rock-cut architecture and water conduit system, Petra is also called the Rose City due to the color of the stone out of which it is carved. It has been a UNESCO World Heritage site since 1985. Petra is a symbol of Jordan. Tourist numbers peaked at one million in 2010, then witnessed a slump due to regional instability. Tourist numbers picked up surpassing one million in 2019.

The Jordan mission concluded with four more days of discussions, which included representatives of the United Nations Refugee Agency and USAID, and visits to the University Hospital and the Military Hospital. It happened to be the month of Ramadan during this visit, and one of the team members was stopped by police and asked not to chew gum.

On June 29 we left Amman to fly to Tunisia for a ten-day mission. The team's schedule included visits to regional hospitals in the capitals of the governorates, starting with Tunis and following the Mediterranean coastline with stops in Sousse, Monastir, Sfax, and Gabès, and then crossing the country westward to Tozeur, at the border with Algeria. Highlights from this trip include: the Roman amphitheater in El Djem, built during the first half of the third century AD—it was quite incongruous to suddenly see a Roman amphitheater in a Muslim country; the domes of the Great Mosque of Kairouan, which was built in 670 and is the oldest mosque in the Maghreb countries; and the Cathedral of Saint Vincent de Paul, a Roman Catholic church located in Tunis and dedicated to Saint Vincent de Paul, patron saint of charity. It is the episcopal see of the Archdiocese of Tunis.

Can silence be heard? Chott el Djerid is a large salt lake in southern Tunisia with a typical hot desert climate. Water evaporates from the lake, and in summer it is almost entirely dry. We crossed the lake in our rental car to reach the western city of Tozeur. We stopped in the evening in the midst of this desert lake. Never before and never again have I experienced a total silence. The dry salt lake has no vegetation, no flora, no fauna, no birds—only total silence. Surreal.

Tozeur is a large oasis with hundreds of thousands of palm trees. Tourism is heavily developed and promoted, and Tozeur is considered a center of "desert tourism." Modern hotels host conferences and tourists arrive at the Tozeur–Nefta International Airport with international services from London, Paris, and Rome.

I left Tunisia by boat to Naples, Italy, on Sunday, July 9 spending three days visiting Naples and Florence before flying home on a Pan Am flight on Wednesday, July 20, concluding a long thirty-six-day trip—the longest I had ever taken so far.

I went back to Tunisia for one-week in September, followed by five days in France. I visited the hospital in Versailles and met with executives of the Hospital Association of Paris, then flew to Bordeaux for another hospital visit. On Wednesday evening, I flew to Belgium to meet with colleagues from the Catholic University of Leuven on Thursday and with colleagues of the Francophone equivalent of the same university on Friday before returning home on Monday, October 3.

My division chief, Stephen Denning, asked me to organize a management training session for the staff and sent me on a one-day trip to Boston to meet with Professor Jim Austin at the Harvard Business School. The five-hour training program by Jim Austin took place on October 19.

Adjusting to the new work environment was stressful—always wanting to prove myself and provide the best quality work I was capable of. Now that we were living in the Washington metropolitan area, we discovered the Arena Stage, the Kennedy Center, and the National Mall, with its monuments and museums.

1984: Colombia, Brazil, Peru, Ecuador, Chile

The previous year, operational work had been focused on the MENA region, with only one mission to a LAC country. This pattern reversed itself in 1984, with a focus on LAC countries and not one MENA assignment. The main reason for this change was the fact that I had been a team member, and now I was the task team leader (TTL) for Colombia, organizing and leading missions and selecting my team members. My fluency in the Spanish language was an asset.

In 1984 I was on travel status for nineteen weeks, making seven trips. To stay within budget the WB assigned country visits back-to-back, meaning that one trip would cover two or sometimes three countries. The first back-to-back three-week trip, from January 16 to February 6, included five days in Colombia, six days in São Paulo, Brazil, and one week in the Brazilian state of Rondônia. The five days in Bogotá were mainly to meet my Colombian partners at the Ministry of Health and reach agreement on a health sector development program. I joined the São Paulo team to supervise the hospital project that I had worked on in 1982. Rondônia is nestled in northwest Brazil, with Porto Velho as its capital city, and the WB-financed project was aimed at controlling the malaria epidemic. Oscar Echeverri was the malaria specialist on the team. Slash-and-burn farming and deforestation for timber export and to increase agricultural land contributed to the breeding grounds and spread of malaria by the infected female *Anopheles* mosquito. The climate is hot and humid all year round, with sudden, short, and heavy rainfalls.

The next three-week trip in March to Colombia included visiting the Valle del Cauca Department, with its capital city Cali and Buenaventura on the Pacific coast. Using outboard motorboats to reach isolated health centers was a new experience. My division chief, Stephen Denning, joined me on this mission.

The longest, seven-week assignment covered Colombia, Brazil, Peru, and Ecuador, from June 17 to August 4. In Colombia I continued to learn to know the country and traveled south to the city of Ipiales, in the Department of Nariño. Ipiales sits on the border with Ecuador, at an elevation of about 2,896 meters (9,500 feet). One of the area's favorite foods is the guinea pig, or cavy, called *kuy*. We spent the weekend in a rustic cabana at the Laguna de la Cocha, famous for its delicious *trucha rosada*, or rainbow trout. La Cocha, a crater lake, is about 16 miles from Nariño's capital, Pasto, and in the middle of the lake is Corota Island, home to a national wildlife sanctuary. We headed back north for a four-day stop in Bogotá, then on to Medellin for three days, returning to Bogotá for a debriefing with the Ministry of Health before leaving for Brazil.

The Brazil portion of this mission was very educational. First, it was my first stay in the capital city, Brasília. Brasília was planned and developed by Lúcio Costa and Oscar Niemeyer in 1956 to move the capital from Rio de Janeiro to a more central location. The city's design divides it into numbered blocks as well as sectors for specified activities, such as the hotel sector, the banking sector, and the embassy sector (with 124 foreign embassies). Brasília was chosen as a UNESCO World Heritage site due to its modernist architecture and uniquely artistic urban planning. All three branches of Brazil's federal government are centered in the city: executive, legislative, and judiciary. Nonetheless, it is not one of my favorite Brazilian cities.

On this trip I also visited the capitals of four of the nine states in the Northeast Region of Brazil: Pernambuco (Recife), Rio Grande do Norte (Natal), Bahia (Salvador), and Sergipe (Aracaju). Most of the states are along the Atlantic coast. To this day, culture in Northeast Brazil, also known as Nordeste, remains permeated by African influence. It was the first area of discovery in Brazil, when roughly 1,500 Portuguese arrived on April 22, 1500, in the state of Bahia. The region's economy is based on coffee, sugarcane, livestock, manufacturing, and textiles, and tourism has grown significantly in the last decades. The tourist industry is based largely on the beaches, which attract thousands of tourists per year, not only from other regions of Brazil but also many from Europe, the United States, and Australia.

From the vibrant Northeast we headed back to Brasília for two days of debriefing and then on to São Paulo for a brief visit. Flying to Lima, Peru, was a side trip not on my official WB schedule. I spent three days in Cusco, the historic capital of the Inca Empire, with its elevation around 3,400 meters (11,200 feet), and visited Machu Picchu for the second time, the fifteenth-century Inca citadel located in the Eastern Cordillera of southern Peru, on a mountain ridge 2,430 meters (7,970 feet) above sea level. The large number of tourists visiting this popular tourist destination has now required visit limits. In 2019 three visiting time slots were imposed: 6:00 a.m. to 9:00 a.m.; 9:00 a.m. to noon; noon to 3:00 p.m. Tickets are valid for four hours and prices vary according to the time slot selected, with the early morning slot being more expensive.

From Lima I flew to Guayaquil, Ecuador to spend a weekend with my former student and friend Wilson Cueva, continuing on for three days of meetings in Quito and returning Saturday, August 4, to Washington, D.C. This was a very long but exciting and educational trip, with the added bonus of time off in Peru and Ecuador.

Three more trips to Colombia as task team leader consisted of one week in October, twelve days in November, and two weeks bridging November and December to reach a final agreement on the structure, objectives, content, and cost of a health project to be financed by the WB, allowing me to prepare the documents for approval of the loan amount by the WB board. On one trip I traveled north to Bucaramanga, which is the capital and largest city of the Department of Santander and a major commercial hub in northeastern Colombia. It is also known for its giant ants that are roasted and eaten as a delicacy (*hormigas tostadas*). I also discovered Melgar, only sixty miles from Bogotá, whose warmer climate makes it a popular weekend destination with temperatures ranging between 28–35° Celsius (82–95 °F). It is an inland resort favored by people of Bogotá on weekends to flee the capital's cold weather.

The University of Chile invited me for a conference and lectures the week of October 15. My major presentation was on how to conduct health services research, and my lectures dealt with approaches to evaluate patient care quality. On Saturday, my hosts drove me to the South Pacific seaport of Valparaíso and to Viña del Mar, which is the most popular beach resort in the country that teems with tourists during peak months December, January, and February, despite Antarctic currents that make swimming a formidable challenge.

It was a good year overall. I enjoyed working in Latin America, making friends, getting to know the countries from the inside, inserting some sightseeing trips in a busy schedule, and feeling that I was beginning to contribute to countries in their efforts to develop their health sectors. Travel may appear to have been overwhelming but accounted only for one third of the year.

1985 and 1986 and a New President at the World Bank: Colombia, Ecuador, Brazil, Chile, Argentina, Mexico

The next two years witnessed a continuation of my work in Latin America, with two trips to Colombia as task team leader (TTL); adding responsibility for health projects in Ecuador and Argentina as a TTL; and being a team member for the health projects in Brazil, Mexico, and Chile.

One of the highlights was visiting the state of Paraíba in Brazil. João Pessoa, its capital, was founded in 1585 and is known as the city where the sun rises first, because it is the easternmost city in the Americas.

Another highlight was traveling to the south of Colombia to the town of Leticia, the southernmost city in Colombia and the capital of the Department of Amazonas as well as one of the major ports on the Amazon River. Leticia has long been Colombia's shipping point for tropical fish for the aquarium trade. Leticia sits on the left bank of the Amazon River at the point where Colombia, Brazil, and Peru come together in an area called Tres Fronteras (Triple Frontier).

Argentina won the soccer World Cup in 1986 in Mexico by beating Germany 3-2 thanks to the genius of Diego Maradona. I arrived in Buenos Aires the day after the championship victory and landed in the midst of a city covered in blue and gone crazy, with nonstop partying.

The Cajón del Maipo In Chile is a canyon in the outskirts of the Andes, southeast of Santiago. The purpose of this visit was to see the place where the unsuccessful attempt was made to kill Chile's dictator Augusto Pinochet.

One week in Mexico served to discuss research topics with future colleagues Julio Frenk, Enrique Ruelas, and Jose Maria Bobadilla. Sadly, Jose Maria perished years later in a plane that crashed in the sea upon taking off from Lima on its way to Santiago.

The Mexican public health journal published my article: "Sinopsis de los planteamientos para evaluar la calidad de la atención al paciente." *Salud Pública de México*, 1986; 28: 221–229.

In 1986 the presidency of the World Bank was passed on from Alden Clausen to Barber Conable. Clausen had succeeded Robert McNamara in 1981 and had previously been the CEO of the Bank of America. Conable had been a U.S. congressman from New York State but had lost his re-election bid. He was recommended by President Reagan to succeed Clausen. Conable was not an expert in banking or international development and contracted with a consulting firm to restructure the World Bank to make it perform more efficiently. The restructuring plan consisted of managers selecting their staff (i.e., the president selects his vice presidents, the vice presidents select their directors, the directors select their division chiefs, and the division chiefs select the professional staff). This was referred to by the staff as "Conable's cascading cronies." Staff who were not selected would receive a generous separation package, and some went into hiding in order *not* to be selected and benefit from the separation bonus. I was fortunate to receive calls from five division chiefs inviting me to join their staff and was in the enviable position of making a choice. There were some division chiefs whom I did not want to work for, as their management skills were known to be lacking.

Managers at the World Bank at any level were often not selected for their management skills. Appointments to manage a division, a department, a region, or to become a vice president were partially influenced by diversity goals, lobbying by national leaders to appoint a staff person from their country, personal preferences of higher-ups, or rewarding staff for outstanding technical skills. The president was always an American citizen proposed by the U.S. president who was invariably ratified by the board of directors. Here, too, management experience was not a top priority. This led in 2005 to the highly controversial selection of Paul Wolfowitz by President George W. Bush. As deputy secretary of defense (2001–2005), Wolfowitz had strongly supported and defended the invasion of Iraq. When pushed aside in 2005 by President Bush (or by Defense Secretary Rumsfeld) he became president of the World Bank to the dismay of the vast majority of the staff. His tenure lasted only two years of the five-year term. He had divorced in 2002 and his girlfriend worked for the WB. They agreed that it would be better for her to resign, and he instructed the human relations vice president to give her an overly generous financial separation package that went against WB rules. The controversy over this favorable treatment led to his resignation in 2007.

I chose to stay in LAC mainly because I liked the division chief, Peter Eigen, but also important was the fact that the director of the department, Pieter Bottelier, called me in for an interview and invited me to join his department. Being wanted by the division chief and his boss made all the difference.

Over the years at the World Bank, Peter Eigen realized how much his work was being dwarfed by the devastating effects of corruption, which in fact he found to be the main obstacle to economic, social, and democratic development. He considered tackling corruption as a vital goal of his work at the World Bank. Eigen was however ordered not to further pursue these efforts, even during his private spare time. The Bank's policy was indeed to regard corruption as part of the internal political and cultural affairs of the respective countries and under its Charter the Bank was not to interfere. Frustrated, Eigen left the World Bank in 1993 and in February of that year he gathered some 20 inspired like-minded experts from around the world in the Hague Netherlands where they signed the Founding Charter of Transparency International (TI). Peter chaired the Board of Directors of TI until 2005. The World Bank reversed its position on corruption under the presidency of James Wolfensohn supporting a global fight against corruption.

1987: Ecuador, Colombia, Chile, Haiti, Argentina, Mexico

Work in Latin America continued with travel to Ecuador, Brazil twice, Chile twice, Colombia twice, Argentina, and Mexico.

My trip to Ecuador included a weekend in the town Otavalo, which is two hours north of Quito and world-famous for its indigenous population. At the Mercado Artesanal, indigenous and mestizo people from Otavalo and surrounding villages sell their handicrafts: weavings, jewelry, clothes, wood and stone carvings, paintings, Panama hats, and some products from neighboring Peru and Colombia. Saturday is the main market day and the whole town is filled with little stalls. During a visit to San Antonio de Ibarra, known as the wood-carving capital of Ecuador, I bought a three-foot-high wooden sculpture representing an old Indian and paid twenty dollars. The challenge was to transport it back to the U.S. I ordered a wooden box made by a carpenter in Quito that turned out to be more expensive than the sculpture itself. Customs agents at Minneapolis–Saint Paul Airport examined the wooden sculpture in agonizing detail, convinced that it contained drugs and not believing that it was one solid piece of wood. This was a nerve-racking moment, watching them poking their knives in a piece of art.

One of my Colombia missions started in Cali and Tuluá (known for its salsa dancing), south of Bogotá, and continued north to the city of Barranquilla, near the Caribbean Sea. Its port was an entry point for immigrants from Europe, especially during and immediately following World War I and World War II. Gabriel García Márquez, Nobel Prize for Literature in 1982, wrote his first novella, *Leaf Storm* (*La Hojarasca*), in Barranquilla. First published in 1955, it took seven years to find a publisher. It is widely celebrated as the first appearance of the fictitious village Macondo, later made famous in *One Hundred Years of Solitude*. Shakira, the Colombian singer, songwriter, and dancer, was born and raised Barranquilla.

The purpose of the three-week stay in Chile was to help the WB team headed by the country economist (Richard Newfarmer) in designing a two-year, $200 million structural adjustment loan that incorporated health outcomes as a conditionality for disbursing the second tranche of $100 million at the end of the first year. This was an impossible task, as it is extremely difficult to develop health performance indicators that would document significant changes in the health sector in the span of one year. One short-term measure I proposed was a prohibition of advertising tobacco products on television. The Chilean negotiators objected to this indicator. The brother-in-law of one of the three military junta members owned a tobacco factory. Agreed-upon health performance indicators became part of the legal documents, but at the end of the first year, vague statements were made that "progress" had been made on these indicators and therefore the disbursement of the second $100 million tranche could proceed. The WB wanted to make the loan and Chile wanted to receive the loan, and acceptable language was found to enable the transaction. This was a disappointing experience.

I visited Haiti for the first time for one week in June. The AIDS virus had been identified in 1983, and Haiti was one of the Caribbean countries hit hard by the virus. Our knowledge of the disease, its etiology, its evolution, its diagnostic testing, and treatment was still quite rudimentary. The minister of health was seeking financing to build a "hospice" in the capital where infected people would be segregated. Despite our limited knowledge of the disease, this was not an acceptable negotiating position. The minister was adamant, and we did not reach an agreement. About fifteen years later I became totally immersed in designing and financing HIV/AIDS projects in the Caribbean region. It took that long for the world development community to recognize and combat AIDS as a global pandemic.

Argentina went through a major financial crisis in 1987. I was part of a two-week mission that included the country economist and the department director, Pieter Bottelier, for several days, and the WB president, Barber Conable, for one day. I did not participate in the high-level negotiations for a bailout financial package between the WB and the country's highest echelons but continued work on a health project. On this trip I travelled north to visit the Iguazú Falls from the Argentine side. I had earlier visited the waterfalls from the Brazil side and the two sides offer a different but equally spectacular sight. They make up the largest waterfall system in the world. The Iguazú River forms the boundary between Argentina and Brazil, but most of the falls are on the Argentine side.

On the return night flight, the WB president and I were seated in first class and Mr. Bottelier, my director, who had changed his travel date at the last minute, was seated in economy class. I was uncomfortable with this seating arrangement and offered respectfully to switch seats with him, but he categorically refused.

1988: Argentina, Ecuador, Uruguay, Chile

The year started out with a long weekend, as Washington, D.C., closed down for a snow day on Friday, January 8. The year included four trips to Argentina and two to Ecuador. Notwithstanding my love for Latin America, I started thinking about the challenge of working in non-LAC countries, acquiring different and new experiences, by transferring to another region. Anticipating that it could be my last year working on Argentina, I took advantage of exploring and visiting more of the country by traveling west and south of Buenos Aires.

Flying west in March I visited the province of Mendoza, famous as a wine-producing region and its Malbec wines. Rio Negro is the province south of Mendoza with the world-known ski resort of Bariloche. As a WB staff member and mission leader, I was always well received by my local colleagues and enjoyed their hospitality, combining health sector–related meetings and discussions with tourist excursions.

The second and third missions to Argentina focused on the implementation of the health project. Both were two weeks in duration, one in June and one in September, each time with meetings in Buenos Aires. This city is frequently referred to as the cultural capital of Latin America, and it does honor to its reputation. The Colón Theater is a majestic and beautifully decorated building that hosts major cultural events. I went to a symphony concert by a Russian orchestra and still remember vividly how they opened with Beethoven's Fifth Symphony in complete darkness. Goose pimples! A colleague (Alicia Garcia Bates) who worked for the City of Buenos Aires Health Department was allowed to use the mayor's theater box. Other shows were the then-famous comedy-musical group Les Luthiers and the internationally known Brazilian singer Gal Costa. Theaters abounded in the city, and I went often to see a theater production.

The fourth trip, however, was the most impressive one, as it took me to the southern tip of the continent, known as Tierra del Fuego. Prior to reaching this point, I visited the province of Santa Cruz, which is part of the Patagonia region. Few places on planet Earth are as remote and untouched as Patagonia. This sparsely populated region, which spans the southernmost tips of Argentina and Chile, is famous for its soaring Andean peaks, windswept steppes, large glaciers, and gaucho culture. We flew from Buenos Aires to Comodoro Rivadavia, a city in the Patagonian province of Chubut that is a commercial and transportation center for the surrounding region and importantly exports Argentine petroleum. A 1,770-kilometer (1,100-mile) pipeline carries natural gas to Buenos Aires. Much of Patagonia is characterized by strong westerlies that are prevailing winds, and Patagonia is dominated by strong winds throughout the year. I found it quite uncomfortable to feel a constant wind, but my colleagues at the health center told me that one gets used to it and one doesn't notice it after a while.

From there we continued by bus to Los Glaciares National Park, which contains the large Upsala Glacier. It flows from the Southern Patagonian Ice Field, feeding the nearby Perito Moreno Glacier. Though not the biggest glacier in Patagonia, Perito Moreno is easily the most famous, as it creeps forward up to two meters per day, resulting in thunderous roars of cascading ice as it calves truck-sized icebergs into Canal de los Témpanos. This thirty-kilometer-long, five-kilometer-wide glacier is the photogenic star of many a postcard and one of Argentina's top attractions. Nearby El Calafate is the main hub for lodgings and tourist services in the southern sector of Los Glaciares National Park, which I visited on a boat ride, even spotting a condor. Fortunately, a Buenos Aires colleague had lent me a down jacket that kept me warm.

Tierra del Fuego is an archipelago off the southernmost tip of the South American mainland, across the Strait of Magellan. Ushuaia is the capital of Tierra del Fuego and is regarded as the southernmost city in the world. It is located in a wide bay on the southern coast of Isla Grande de Tierra del Fuego, bordered on the north by the Martial Mountain range and on the south by the Beagle Channel.

Several ski areas are located near Ushuaia, including Glacier El Martial and Cerro Castor, which is the southernmost ski resort in the world. On Cerro Castor, it is possible to ski just 200 meters (660 feet) above sea level. The summit reaches an elevation of 1,003 meters (3,291 feet) and consistently cool temperatures allow the longest skiing season in South America. Winter temperatures fluctuate between 0 and minus 5 degrees Celsius (32 to 23 degrees Fahrenheit). It has twenty-eight ski trails for all skill levels. There are cafeterias, mountain huts, a ski school, a first-aid room, and a forest of beech trees. Snowboarding, sledding, and snowshoeing are also available at Cerro Castor, in addition to Alpine skiing.

Daylight in summer averages twenty-two hours a day and, conversely, in winter it is dark twenty-two hours a day. So, my first meeting with the provincial director of health was in clear daylight at ten o'clock in the evening. A bit incongruous to have coffee served and discuss the health issues of the province at that time of day. The province has difficulty attracting and retaining a quality health workforce. It is especially hard on married couples when one partner is not employed. Imagine a day with only two hours of daylight. Depression is common, and turnover of staff is high.

This trip to the southern edge of the continent was part of my last and longest mission to South America. I had left Washington on October 23 for one week in Quito, Ecuador; continued to Buenos Aires, Argentina, for two weeks; went to Santiago, Chile, for four days; returned to Buenos Aires to go west and south as described above; then traveled to Asunción, Uruguay, on November 27 for a visit with friends on my way to Porto Alegre, Brazil, where I arrived on Friday, December 2, for one week with the

Belgian family of my brother-in-law, finally returning home on December 10.

An interesting occurrence during my May 16–27 trip to Ecuador is worth telling. Roberto Bobenrieth, brother of my "compadre" Manuel, was a veterinarian on the staff of PAHO based in Quito. Roberto had been invited to the mountain home of the renowned and internationally acclaimed Ecuadorean painter Oswaldo Guayasamín (1919–1999), a master painter and sculptor of Quechua and Mestizo heritage. Roberto asked me to go with him and we visited his workshop, chatted with him, and shared a cup of coffee. I purchased a set of four drawings known as the "hands and faces series" in which a pair of hands expresses strong emotions such as protest and terror. I still have the drawings and the receipt, dated May 21, 1988, for a total of 2,500 pesos.

My Chilean friend Jorge Jimenez had been active in opposing the Pinochet dictatorship. I had worked with Jorge during an earlier trip to Chile assisting in preparing the national health program to be implemented once democracy was restored. That visit had been requested by the WB country economist (Paul Meo) under the guise of technical assistance to a research program that Jorge Jimenez and Jorge Hernandez were carrying out through a catholic NGO. Actually, the WB saw the end of the Pinochet regime coming and wanted to establish relationships with the eventual successors. During the day I was a member of the research team, and in the evenings, we discussed future health policies. Jorge was in the crosshairs of the Pinochet regime, and it was safer for him to leave the country for a while. He received an Eisenhower Fellowship to study at Johns Hopkins University in Baltimore. The scholarship only paid a meager $900 a month, and my division chief Peter Eigen arranged to recruit him as a consultant for a lump sum of $5,000. I was asked to figure out a work program to justify the consultant fee, so I asked Jorge to write a report analyzing the health sector in Peru.

Ironically, I became formally his supervisor for this assignment, which he completed successfully.

The democratic elections of 1989 replaced the Pinochet dictatorship, and Jorge was appointed minister of health in the new democratic government. Jorge Hernandez became deputy minister of finance. Two years into Jorge's tenure as minister of health, the country faced a doctors' strike damaging to the public's view of the country's president. What usually happens under those circumstances is a presidential decision to show strength and to fire the minister of health. The president removed Jorge from office and appointed him as the country's ambassador to Italy. I visited the large, beautifully decorated embassy on a later stay in Rome and had a superb dinner with Jorge and his wife, Margarita, in one of the Monti neighborhood restaurants.

At this point I became active in pursuing my objective of changing regions. After the 1987 reorganization, the WB had created technical departments in each of the six geographic regions that would house a talent pool to serve the operational divisions in each region. My goal was set on the East Asia and Pacific (EAP) region, and my first interview with the division chief of the EAP Technical Department (Alex ter Weele) was on August 22 when I also met his director Amnon Golan. Subsequently, I met with the division chief responsible for China (Zafer Ecevit) and the division chief managing projects in Laos, Thailand, and South Korea (Brad Babson, later replaced by Shiva Kumar upon Brad's promotion to director). My transfer was approved on January 1, 1989.

Transferring to the East Asia and Pacific Region in 1989: Laos, China, South Korea

I moved offices from the I Building on I Street NW to the D Building in the main WB complex on H Street NW. My new office looked out on 19th Street NW and the IMF building. As a Task team leader, I was assigned responsibility for projects in South Korea, Laos, and China and worked with these countries until my retirement in 1997. Retirement age was officially sixty-two, meaning that I would retire in 1994. A request for an exception to the rule was submitted by my division chief, Jim Socknat, and approved by the technical department director, Daniel Ritchie, to allow me to continue three more years. This exception required a signature from the vice president of human resources. I wanted to continue working on the projects I had initiated, and I enjoyed my work. Equally important was adding three years of service that would increase the amount of my future pension.

I worked with these three countries for eight years, and the juxtaposition of them would cause a cultural shock on each trip. Flying from Laos, one of the poorest countries in the world with a per capita income of US$190 to South Korea, an upper-middle-income country, with a per capita income of about US$5,000, was indeed shocking. Or flying from Laos, which had 4 million inhabitants, to China, with 1.2 billion people, was always equally impressive.

Traveling four times a year to these countries is a physical challenge, as flying and connecting times are long- and the time difference is twelve hours. I tried initially to break up the trip by using an authorized stopover in Hawaii, but the hassle of checking into a hotel and checking out the next day was stressful and not helpful to counter the jetlag. The newness of landing in Hawaii with the opportunity to stay an extra day to visit the island and the volcanoes was attractive, but soon wore off. Hawaii is a favorite honeymoon destination for Japanese newlyweds. Deck chairs are tightly arranged around the swimming pool at the Sheraton. At six o'clock in the morning, Japanese couples had already put a personal item on a deck chair, reserving it for the day.

Next, I switched to a stopover either in Tokyo or Hong Kong after a twelve-hour flight. The preference became Hong Kong, with an airport closer to downtown with connecting flights to

Bangkok, Seoul, or Beijing, and being a bustling, lively city. Flying to Laos required another five-hour flight from Hong Kong to Bangkok and then a one-hour flight from Bangkok to Vientiane, Laos's capital, often the next day, as there was only one flight a day to Vientiane. Door to door this would take thirty-six hours of travel. Nowadays there are direct nonstop flights from Washington, D.C., to Beijing. Flying via Europe with a stopover would have been more accommodating, as it cuts the time difference into two segments of six hours. However, this would be more expensive, and the WB did not allow us to travel eastward.

LAOS

Laos is a socialist state and the only landlocked country in Southeast Asia. It is bordered by Myanmar (Burma) and China to the northwest, Vietnam to the east, Cambodia to the southwest, and Thailand to the west and southwest. Laos was a French colony part of French Indochina. It provided a supply route for North Vietnam during the Vietnam War and the United States responded with a bombing campaign Laos became the Lao People's Democratic Republic at the end of the Vietnam War in 1975 with the abdication of the Lao king and the victory of the Pathet Lao communist army. Lao's recent history was very much evident in 1989, when responsibility for assistance to develop the health sector was handed over to me by my colleague Bernhard Liese.

In 1989 Laos had a population of 4.26 million, a life expectancy of fifty-four years, a GNP per capita of US$190, and was one of the poorest countries in the world. Government salary was about US$100 per month and the monthly salary of the minister of health was US$300.

The older generation of the educated social class had been trained in France and spoke French fluently. The minister of health, Dr. Vannereth, had graduated from a French medical school and we always conversed in French. American assistance in health matters, according to the American ambassador whom I interviewed, only consisted of making available medical specialists and technicians to provide prosthetic devices to farmers along the North Vietnamese border who had lost extremities stepping on land mines.

Another area still covered with unexploded bombs is the Plain of Jars, one of the most important prehistoric sites in Southeast Asia, which dates to the Iron Age. Scattered over hundreds of square miles across the mountains surrounding Phonsavan, in northeastern Laos, are thousands of giant stone jars thought to have been used as funeral urns. Between 1964 and 1973, the Plain of Jars was heavily bombed by the U.S. Air Force. The U.S. Air Force dropped more bombs on Laos, primarily the Plain of Jars, than it dropped during the whole of World War II, including 262 million anti-personnel cluster bombs. An estimated 80 million of these did not explode and remain a deadly threat. The large quantity of unexploded bombs in the area, especially cluster munitions, limits free movement. Evidence of the bombing raids can still be seen by the broken jars and bomb craters. Sightseeing on the Plain of Jars is only on cleared and marked pathways.

Laos's infrastructure in most sectors was not functioning in 1989. There was one government-owned and run hotel in the capital city, Vientiane—Lane Xang Hotel—and having a reservation did not guarantee that you would have a room. The private sector was absent. Loudspeakers on each street corner blasted communist messages at 6:00 a.m. and in the evening, when streets were dark and mostly empty. There were two telephone landlines for incoming and outgoing calls. To make a call one would go to the telephone office, request a call, and stand in line. Over the span of eight years that I worked with the country, it was fascinating to watch Vientiane wake up from its communist dream and slowly evolve into a vibrant city. Private sector activities were allowed, resulting in more hotels, more restaurants, small shops on the main streets, vendors along the Mekong River, more cars, and, especially, more scooters.

The tourism sector began to grow rapidly, from 80,000 international visitors in 1990 to 1.9 million in 2010, with one in every ten jobs being in the tourism sector. Some of the main attractions include the Buddhist culture and colonial architecture in Luang Prabang and ancient temples in Vientiane. The population in 2022 has grown to 7.5 million, life expectancy has increased to 68 years, and the GNP per capita was up to US$2,088, classifying the country as a lower middle-income country and no longer a low-income country.

The World Bank had already financed a factory that was producing textile products when I started work in Laos. Health and education were also priority sectors. It took four years to have a health project approved by the country and the board of directors of the WB. The US$19.2 million, six-year project was financed by a soft loan, meaning no interest payments, with forty years' maturity and ten years of grace before starting to repay the principal. The long maturity of a soft loan coupled with inflation effectively results in a 70 percent grant.

The health project's objectives were to: (a) improve the quality of basic health care, particularly for infants, children, and women, as infant and maternal mortality rates were very high; and (b) strengthen the malaria control program in the country, as malaria was endemic and a major cause of death, especially for children. Savannakhet and Sekong were selected as pilot provinces to implement priority health programs. The project design was highly participative, involving Lao counterparts in workshops to ensure country ownership of the World Bank–financed project. This approach was described in a chapter of *The World Bank Participation Sourcebook*, published in 1996.

Savannakhet with 16 percent of the total population was the country's most populous province. Its thirteen districts and 1,602 villages are a microcosm of the entire country, due to a high degree of variation in terms of geography, socioeconomic variables, and ethnicity. About 80 percent of its income comes from agriculture. Western Savannakhet is part of the Mekong Valley bordering Thailand. The eastern part borders Vietnam and is mountainous, with many inaccessible villages inhabited by ethnic minority groups, reachable only four months per year.

Sekong had a population of 59,000 (1.4 percent of total country) and was the least populated and newest province. Created in 1984, it was inhabited by fourteen ethnic groups, each with its own native tongue. Its estimated per capita income was US$140. Two districts had an average village size of 133 people, were difficult to access year-round, and were completely cut off during the rainy season. About 95 percent of the population were illiterate, putting a severe constraint on recruiting and training local people. Personnel from other provinces were very reluctant to work in Sekong due to its remoteness, and turnover was high. We traveled to Sekong by flying in a rickety airplane to Pakse, capital of Champasak, the southernmost province bordering Cambodia, and then driving east by jeep.

Remnants of the French influence was still evident when staying overnight in Pakse, with a delicious baguette and café au lait for breakfast. A typical Lao breakfast would be a hearty rice soup with fish or chicken. The distance from Pakse to Sekong was only one hundred miles, but it took seven hours on a potholed and dusty road in a bare-bones Toyota jeep with no air-conditioning. Dust invaded the open windows, painting us red. Upon arrival, we dove into the river for the most refreshing bath I had ever taken. Lodging was in a government guesthouse, which was a wooden structure on stilts with rooms that slept eight people, with malaria nets over each bed. Use of the outhouse required filling a bucket of water at a standpipe, and washing in the morning was done by pumping water into the same bucket. On a later trip we were able to stay in the house used by a French NGO called Action Contre la Faim.

We flew north once to visit Luang Prabang well known for its numerous Buddhist temples and monasteries. Every morning, hundreds of monks from the various monasteries walk through the streets with their bowls collecting food. One of the city's major landmarks is Mount Phou Si, a steep hill of 490 feet, which we climbed. This steep staircase leads to Wat Chom Si shrine and an impressive view of the city and the rivers.

The country's plentiful water resources and mountainous terrain enable it to produce and export large quantities of hydroelectric energy, which is sold to neighboring Thailand and Vietnam and is a major source of national income. This means building dams flooding large areas of land, including villages. Swimming in a dammed area among flooded trees was eerie and exciting.

CHINA

My first visit to China was scheduled for June 1989. In early June I was in Laos, ready to fly to Beijing, when I started receiving telegrams from the Thai WB office in Bangkok and from Washington, D.C., headquarters ordering me to return immediately and not to proceed to China. I didn't know the reason why, as we had no access to international news. The harsh repression of the student protests at Tiananmen Square had occurred on June 4 in Beijing, and the WB recalled all staff in China or scheduled to arrive in China.

The Tiananmen Square protests, commonly known in mainland China as the June Fourth Incident, were student-led demonstrations in Beijing. The protests were forcibly suppressed after Chinese Premier Li Peng declared martial law. In what became known in the West as the Tiananmen Square Massacre, troops with automatic rifles and tanks fired at demonstrators who were trying to block the military's advance toward Tiananmen Square. Conflicting estimates put the number of civilian deaths between 180 and 10,454.

My first travel to China took place in October 1989. China's government was anxious to restore its damaged image and was extremely courteous toward foreign visitors. We received an invitation at the hotel to attend a performance at the Great Hall of the People on October 1, Chinese National Day. A minibus collected us at the hotel. The performance turned out to be a series of bombastic operatic pieces glorifying the Communist Party, its leader, the military, and patriotism using historical and modern themes. We were then guided to a viewing stand on Tiananmen Square to watch the fireworks commemorating the founding of the People's Republic of China in 1949. China's fireworks are spectacular and were the best I had ever seen. It was a very cold evening, though, sitting on the concrete benches and not dressed appropriately.

One vivid recollection of my first arrival in China was walking out of the Beijing airport and seeing a large billboard of the Marlboro man. I was amazed, shocked, and intrigued.

The next sixteen trips to China revolved around the design and approval of a health project and assessing its implementation progress. The goal of the health project was to upgrade the clinical skills of rural health workers to improve the health status of the rural poor in six provinces: Guizhou, Anhui, Henan, Shanxi, Hebei, and Fujian. The project would strengthen workforce planning; train and retrain medical teachers, rural health workers, and managers; emphasize training in clinical skills needed to treat patients in rural settings; and upgrade the physical conditions of training and service delivery institutions at the county, township, and village levels.

WB financing for the project, called the Rural Health Workers Development Project, was approved on July 12, 1993. Financing was a US$110 million credit with no interest and with thirty-five years' maturity. The combined population of the six targeted provinces was around 200 million people. The genesis of the project derives from a 1990 nationwide sample survey. A discussion of the findings of the survey are reported in the World Bank Technical Paper No. 187: "From Barefoot Doctor to Village Doctor in Rural China: From Collectivization to Privatization of Rural Health Care," 1992, by Willy De Geyndt, Xiyan Zhao, and Shunli Liu.

The survey documented the increasing concern of the national and provincial authorities about the low level of clinical training of the rural doctor combined with the vested authority to dispense potent and expensive Western drugs, and about the neglect of preventive public health measures.

The profile of the average Chinese village doctor that emerged from the survey was that of a middle-aged male with less than secondary school education, working part-time as a self-employed doctor, having received less than one year on-the-job or classroom medical training, but with more than fifteen years of hands-on experience, earning more than the average villager by combining income from village doctor practice and from farmwork, and desirous of receiving additional short-term or correspondence training.

Consequences of this profile showed up in the clinical mistakes made by the village doctor: (a) misdiagnosis or inability to diagnose as a result of inadequate training and a lack of basic diagnostic tools; (b) unnecessary or inappropriate prescriptions, such as analgesics for acute abdominal pain, intravenous solutions of amino acids for fatigue, 10 percent instead of 5 percent glucose administered intravenously, antibiotics for nonbacterial infections, adrenocortical hormones for common colds, and dosage errors for children; (c) overprescribing antipyretics, antibiotics (especially gentamycin, kanamycin, erythromycin, and streptomycin), digitalis, and procaine; and (d) poor aseptic techniques: reuse of disposable syringes; sepsis in deliveries for lack of sterilizing instruments, resulting in iatrogenic infections.

The project emphasized training the rural health worker in practical clinical skills needed in rural settings in accord with prevailing pathology. One of several training modes recommended to improve technical competence was task-based teaching and learning, i.e., list the tasks to be carried out according to the pathology encountered in rural settings and focus training on efficiently, effectively, and efficaciously carrying out tasks that reflect the epidemiological reality of the villages. Yet the project was least successful in meeting this goal. Why? Intensive courses or refresher courses offered by county health schools are watered-down preclinical courses in anatomy, pathophysiology, organic chemistry, etc. Provinces are required to test medical workers, and examinations focus on these traditional preclinical courses. Results are published nationally, listing scores obtained by provinces. Competency in carrying out relevant rural tasks as intended by the project could not compete in the national ranking with scores that are based on memorizing textbook material and on provinces competing for a good ranking. On the other hand, the project was successful in improving the physical structure and equipment for training and service-delivery institutions at the county level. Construction and equipment purchases were easily achieved.

An enjoyable task was the visit to each of the six provinces, especially traveling to small villages and townships. We were always very well received as honored guests and offered generous banquets with a variety of food and presents to take home. Having a Chinese-speaking colleague on the team (Shiyan Chao) was extremely helpful. The banquets too often became an occasion for the hosts to drink heavily by inviting each mission member to a toast. Good-natured drinking competitions between adjacent tables are part of the culture. Chinese colleagues seated at other tables would come to the head table to toast. As mission leader, I was always seated at the head table with the local authorities. I became quickly adept at cheating by filling my small glass with water or using valid excuses claiming medical reasons (doctor orders, medications) for abstaining from alcohol. One of my team members—an Australian consultant—once accepted the challenge to empty his glass without flinching, winning with twenty-seven shots bottoms up. He ended up very drunk, and I had a stern talk with him the next day and it did not happen again.

Baijiu is a distilled spirit with an alcohol content greater than 30 percent and is sometimes called "Chinese vodka". There are many varieties, classified by their fragrance, but most are only distilled once, making for stronger flavors and scent than vodka. The prestige brand is the "sauce scented" Moutai. The default toast in China is "*ganbei*," which literally means "dry cup."

The six project provinces were in different parts of the country with their own idiosyncrasies: geography, ethnicity, food, religions, dialects. We drove to one province in a minibus, took an overnight train to one, and an airplane to the other four.

GUIZHOU is demographically one of China's most diverse provinces. It is relatively poor and economically undeveloped, but rich in natural, cultural, and environmental resources. Its per capita GDP is the lowest in China. Minority groups account for more than 37 percent of the population, and 55.5 percent of the province area is designated as autonomous regions for ethnic minorities. I very much remember the dresses and dances of the minority groups and the buffalo horn I was given as a present.

ANHUI is located in the eastern region of the country and had a population of 62 million in 2017. Hefei is the provincial capital. The Yangtze River, the longest river in Asia at 6,380 kilometers (3,964 miles), crosses the province. Huangshan (or Yellow Mountain) is a mountain range in southern Anhui, with trees growing up to the tree line at 1,800 meters (5,900 feet). The Yellow Mountain is well known for its scenery and sunsets, peculiarly shaped granite peaks, pine trees, hot springs, winter snow, and views of the clouds from above. Huangshan is a frequent subject of traditional Chinese paintings and literature, as well as modern photography. It is a UNESCO World Heritage Site, and one of China's major tourist destinations. I was fortunate to stay overnight on the mountain.

HENAN is located in the central part of the country and is China's third most populous province with a population of more than 94 million. If it were a country by itself, Henan would be the fourteenth most populous country in the world. It is the "Midwest" or "breadbasket" of China. The Yellow River, the second longest in Asia, passes through central Henan and causes frequent devastating floods.

SHANXI is in the North China region, and the Great Wall of China forms most of the northern border with Inner Mongolia. The GDP per capita is below the national average. Industry is centered around heavy industries such as coal and chemical production, power generation, and metal refining. It has more coal companies than any other province. Not surprisingly, is it one of the most polluted areas in China. There are also countless military-related industries due to its history as the former base of the Chinese Communist Party and the People's Liberation Army. Its cuisine is most well-known for its extensive use of vinegar as a condiment, as well as for a large variety of noodle dishes.

SHANXI province can be confused with Shaanxi province. Distinguishing the pronunciation of the two names is almost impossible for foreigners but very clear in Chinese. I visited Shaanxi, which is a two-hour flight from Beijing, to see the world-famous Terracotta Army, a collection of life-size terracotta sculptures depicting the armies of Qin Shi Huang, the first emperor of China, including warriors, chariots, and horses. It is presumed to be a form of funerary art buried with the emperor in 210–209 BC with the purpose to protect him in his afterlife. Estimates from 2007 were that the three pits containing the Terracotta Army held more than 8,000 soldiers, 130 chariots with 520 horses, and 150 cavalry horses, the majority of which remained buried in the pits near Qin Shi Huang's mausoleum.

HEBEI is a province in the North China region with a population of 75 million and accessible by car from the capital. The Great Wall crosses the northern part of Hebei, and the eastern end on the coast features the popular beach resort of Beidaihe. Built in 220–206 BC, the entire wall, with all its branches, measures 21,196 kilometers (13,171 miles). We visited a medical school teaching traditional Chinese medicine in the capital city of Shijiazhuang. At the end of one of our site visits, the chief of health services asked us if we wanted to go to a piano bar. We found this a strange request in midafternoon, as we associated a piano bar with drinks, listening to music, and maybe singing, but we courteously accepted the invitation. The piano bar was a room with a piano and a menu of musical pieces that could be requested to be played. The owner, being an opera singer, could be asked to accompany the piano. Tea was served and was free, but the musical pieces on the menu had a price attached to them.

FUJIAN is a province on the southeast coast of mainland China with a population of 37 million. Its capital is Fuzhou. Fujian is separated from Taiwan by the 110-mile-wide Taiwan Strait. Historical Fujian is divided between the People's Republic of China and the Republic of China (or Taiwan), and both territories have a Fujian province in their respective administration divisions. Since the late 1970s, the economy of coastal Fujian has greatly benefited from its geographic and cultural proximity to Taiwan and its Xiamen Free Trade Zone. We were invited to a party by the School of Nursing during one of our project visits. I remember waltzing nursing students to the music of the 1965 movie *Doctor Zhivago*!

I visited Shanghai and two more provinces for academic or tourist reasons. Shanghai is the commercial and financial center of China and falls under the direct administration of the central government. With 25 million people, it is the most populous urban area in China, and the second most populous city proper in the world. I visited Shanghai on two occasions, once for attending a conference and presenting a paper, and once for assessing the progress of a WB-financed health project managed by a WB colleague—noteworthy for already studying antibiotic resistance in the early 1990s. The project had a strong clinical laboratory component with the procurement of relevant equipment. Project officials complained about the WB procurement guidelines forcing them to purchase equipment with the lowest bid. This resulted in the purchase of mostly Chinese-manufactured medical equipment of inferior quality, when what the researchers really wanted were Philips or Siemens products, including service contracts.

I visited Chengdu, in the province of Sichuan, to attend a conference and discuss health policy options with government officials. Sichuan, in the southwest bordering Tibet, is one of China's largest provinces, with a population of 81 million. Its capital city of Chengdu has 14 million people. Sichuan is well known for its spicy cuisine and use of Sichuan peppers, but it is even better known for its giant pandas living in bamboo forests. Most of the panda population lives in Sichuan, and bamboo makes up more than 99 percent of their diet.

For tourist reasons I traveled by train from Chengdu to Kunming, the capital of Yunnan province in southwest China bordering Tibet. Karaoke had become very popular, and one of the train cars offered the opportunity to sing along or alone. Some singers were not very good, and we had to bear with them. The main purpose of this visit was to see the Stone Forest, or Shilin, approximately ninety kilometers (fifty-six miles) from Kunming. The Stone Forest is an area of limestone formations that rise from the ground like stalagmites, with many looking like petrified trees, thereby creating the illusion of a forest made of stone. Some 270 million years ago the Stone Forest area was a shallow sea. It was quite impressive to walk through a forest made of stone.

In summary, working in China with Chinese colleagues, making friends, visiting world-famous tourist destinations, tasting the amazing variety of Chinese food, walking downhill on a narrow path to reach a health clinic in a small village, staying in government housing, showering with only hot water when the cold-water faucet was defective, and enjoying the hospitality at all levels was an unforgettable experience. Hotels in provincial capital cities were comfortable, and the hosts aimed to please—to the point that in one hotel there was a separate section in the restaurant where they served a Western breakfast (fried eggs with toast and coffee) when a Chinese breakfast would have been much tastier.

Professionally, it was easy to work with our Chinese counterparts. They always provided data needed for research and policy analysis, and legally required progress reports were always ready on time. Project timelines never required a time extension. Meetings started and ended on time. Our colleagues at the central level were eager to learn. The language barrier, however, was at times difficult to overcome. Translators at lower levels in the provinces were English teachers, and we learned to adapt and use simple words. A pediatrician would be a "baby doctor" and an obstetrician would be a "doctor for women." I did not allow the Chinese team member, Shiyan Chao, to become a translator; she was on the team as a health economist. When making a presentation, my Chinese colleagues would prepare slides in Mandarin, and the audience would read along with what I was saying in English. Sometimes we used two screens: one in English and one in Mandarin.

SOUTH KOREA

Arriving in Seoul from Laos or from the provinces of China was always a sharp socioeconomic contrast. South Korea at the time was an upper-middle-income country, soon to be admitted to the Organization for Economic Co-operation and Development (OECD), a group of developed countries headquartered in Paris. It was convenient to stay at the Westin Chosun Seoul next to the large department store (Lotte), with restaurants on its top floors and indoor connections to a large underground shopping area.

The executive floor at the hotel offered all needed business services.

My task was to assist in designing a health project partially financed by the WB. The loan for the Public Hospital Modernization Project was approved by the WB on June 29, 1992, in the amount of US$30 million, repayable in fifteen years, including five years of grace. The project would increase access of the rural and urban poor to medical care services, especially for noncommunicable diseases, and improve the quality of medical care in public hospitals. Replacing and adding medical equipment in provincial and municipal hospitals would expand diagnostic and treatment capabilities. For the next four years, I would visit the country twice a year to assess how well project objectives were being achieved. Progress was smooth and on time, and progress reports were always available before each visit.

The project called for numerous visits to urban and rural hospitals, traveling throughout the country, including to Pusan (now Busan) in the south, the country's second largest city. We were always well received, and I enjoyed the hospitality and the discussion and exchange of ideas being always impressed by the high educational standard of our clinical and academic colleagues.

On an aside, the former president of the WB Jim Yong Kim is of Korean descent. Ban Ki-moon, the former secretary-general of the United Nations (from 2007 to 2016), was a South Korean national, as was Youngsoo Shin, the former head of the WHO regional office in Manila. I worked with Dr. Shin in Seoul when he was the president of the Korean Institute of Health Services Management and later met with him in Manila.

The country had reached a per capita income level in the 1990s that no longer qualified it to borrow from the WB. Shortly before this policy took effect, I was still able to prepare one of the last WB lending operations. This second health project incorporated an unusual design that appealed to the WB country economist and to his colleagues who encouraged private sector inclusion. Most hospitals are private (only sixteen are public), and private hospitals had difficulty securing loans from commercial banks. In a booming economy, banks could choose what to invest in. Hospitals were not attractive or priority investments. The design we proposed to WB management would make the loan to the Finance Ministry, which then in turn would lend the money to private hospitals using strict investment banking criteria. This was called an on-lending design. It turned out to be appealing because, first, it would follow WB policy to lend to countries, and second, the loan funds would be disbursed to the private sector, i.e., the private hospitals.

Project preparation included a team member with experience in private banking who met with commercial banks in Seoul and was able to explain the reluctance of banks to lend to hospitals, helping make the case for the proposed on-lending design. This experience was quite different from traditional project designs. However, looking back, I wonder if the lending operation was driven more by ideology than by actual financial need of capital. Private hospitals in South Korea are nonprofit entities yet pay taxes unlike nonprofit entities in other countries. A well-managed private hospital in a country with universal mandatory health insurance should be able to generate funds for its capital needs.

Sundry items that stand out in my recollections are the subordinate status of women e.g. translators would always be females who would never look at men when listening or talking, passing a truck loaded with dog corpses (dog meat will be banned by 2027), moving to your left to pass people, the quality of the Japanese restaurants (Japan occupied Korea for thirty-five years), the discomfort of eating while sitting cross-legged on the floor, not being able to acquire a liking for the famous kimchi food, too many beef dishes, the onset of traffic jams and pollution in Seoul, and exclusively Korean-made cars on the roads.

Other East Asian Travels

JAPAN

Visits to Japan—not counting the stopovers—included Tokyo for professional purposes and Kyoto for tourism. In Tokyo I met with Japan International Cooperation Agency staff to coordinate our health-sector development activities in Laos, where Japan was financing a primary health care project, and for exploring cooperation in other East Asian countries. Other Tokyo trips were for attending a regional congress, presenting a scholarly paper, participating in panels, and meeting with academic colleagues. The Greater Tokyo Area, with over 38 million people, is the world's most populous metropolitan area. Accommodations in prefab hotels with prefab rooms and bathrooms were a novelty. One could spend hours just walking through this bustling city, observing, looking, and eating in small side-street restaurants.

The most exciting trip however was visiting Kyoto, known for being the former imperial capital of Japan for more than one thousand years. The high-speed rail service links Kyoto with Tokyo and takes two hours and eighteen minutes. With its 1,600 Buddhist temples, 400 Shinto shrines, as well as palaces, gardens, and architecture, it is one of the best-preserved cities in Japan. The Japanese maple and weeping willows, the camellia, azalea, and sugar cherry flowers, and the perfectly groomed gardens are a delight.

An unforgettable experience was staying, not in a hotel, but in a *ryokan*, a type of traditional Japanese inn. Bedding is a futon spread out on the tatami floor. Entering your room, you see a table and supplies for making tea. The table is also used for meals when guests take them in their room. While guests are out visiting, staff will move the table and set out the futon for the night's sleep—impeccable service, immersing one fully in a Japanese environment.

THAILAND

Thailand is a country where I combined professional engagements with tourism. The Oriental Hotel in Bangkok was the favorite place to stay for stopovers, for meetings, for tourism, or for scuba diving. It sits on the banks of the Chao Phraya River and is consistently rated by travel magazines as one of the world's top hotels. Being on the river allows one to take a river taxi, avoiding traffic jams.

Regional headquarters of the WB are in Bangkok, with a large staff and communication and meeting facilities. To support the health project in Laos, I recruited Thai consultants, who have the advantage of linguistic and cultural closeness to Laos. I also met with a leading university to program a regional WB flagship course on health systems and health policies.

Laos and Thailand are separated by the Mekong River and ferry boats used to take people across. I took the ferry from Vientiane in Laos to Nong Khai in Thailand where I boarded a train to Bangkok but stopped on the way in Khon Kaen to visit a hospital and a health center. The train ride showed me another side of the geography and people of Thailand. A few years later, the First Thai–Lao Friendship Bridge was built over the Mekong River and ferries became obsolete. Financing came from the Australian government as development aid for Laos. The Second Thai–Lao Friendship Bridge further south at Savannakhet opened in January 2007, intensifying the traffic and commerce between the two countries.

Mae Hong Son is a town in northwest Thailand, in the Shan Hills, near the border with Burma (now Myanmar) along the banks of the river Pai and reached it by bus from Chiang Mai. It is a popular jumping-off point for tours to visit hill tribe villages, caves, and waterfalls.

Among the most "popular" of the hill tribes are the Padaung, commonly referred to as the tribe of "long-necked" women. Girls typically start wearing small coils around their necks at the age of six, and the size of the coil is increased as they grow older. The coils on adults weigh about five kilograms (eleven pounds). The ethics of whether to visit these people is a difficult choice. On one hand, tourism is one of the few ways that these people earn a living. As refugees from Myanmar, they are not allowed to seek regular work in Thailand. Most of the women seem to be proud of their heritage and are not embarrassed to show it off to tourists. On the other hand, it may be perpetuating a form of female mutilation that might otherwise be dying out, and young girls may be pressured into it just to earn money for the family.

The purpose of a short trip to Chanthaburi, a province in the east of Thailand on the border of Cambodia was to learn about

A woman from the Padaung tribe. Girls start wearing the coils to stretch their necks around the age of six.

the primary health care project sponsored by the Antwerp Institute of Tropical Medicine, where one of my Laos team members, Wim Van Lerberghe, had been on the faculty.

Other World Regions

INDIA

In 1992 I was asked to lead a mission to India to review the progress of a health project in the state of Andhra Pradesh, one of the twenty-eight states of India. Andhra Pradesh has a coastline of 974 kilometers (605 miles) on the Bay of Bengal. Hyderabad is the state capital. The Integrated Child Development Services Project aimed at improving the nutrition and health status of children under six years of age, with special emphasis on those less than three years old, and pregnant and nursing women. My colleague Tony Measham had designed and started the project. This mission came at the end of a China mission, so in June 1992 I flew from the world's most populous country to the world's second most populous country. From Beijing we flew to Hyderabad via Hong Kong and Mumbai. After visiting many health centers and rural hospitals, we were invited for dinner at the home of the state's director of health. His wife had prepared for dessert the best mango pie I had ever tasted.

This was my only trip to India and gave me the opportunity to explore the capital of New Delhi and to visit the world-famous Taj Mahal. The ivory-white marble mausoleum in the city of Agra attracts over eight million visitors a year. I also walked through the seventeenth-century Red Fort, with its mass of domes and turrets, and admired the national Indian Gate monument commemorating the Indian soldiers killed in the First World War and built in the triumphal arch style similar to Paris's Arc de Triomphe.

RUSSIA

The USSR had become the independent Russian Federation in December of 1991 with Boris Yeltsin as the first directly elected president in Russian history. I joined a World Bank health project supervision mission led by Elaine Patterson in November 1994. The team split up to visit different regions where the project was active. I was assigned the Smolensk region.

Smolensk is the administrative center of Smolensk Oblast, located on the Dnieper River 360 kilometers (220 miles) west-southwest of Moscow. From July to September 1941 one of the bitterest battles of World War II was fought in and around Smolensk, preventing the Germans from advancing to Moscow before winter. In September 1943 another great battle forced the Germans to abandon the city. The war's damage was still visible in 1994 as reconstruction proceeded.

The five-hour auto ride from Moscow to Smolensk passed by the town of Gagarin, named after Yuri Gagarin, the first human to journey into outer space when his Vostok spacecraft completed one orbit of the Earth on April 12, 1961. This feat prompted President Kennedy to set the goal of a moon landing by the end of the decade.

Accommodations and service in the old and deteriorated government-owned and -run hotel in Smolensk were dreadful, and the rooms were very cold. Heating was centrally produced by the city and piped to all houses. It was November, and the government-set date for distributing heat was December 1. I had experienced a similar schedule in Communist China. Windows did not close tightly, and the lack of heat made working in the hotel room strenuous; I recall struggling to type while wearing gloves.

We visited several health centers and small rural hospitals. This is when I experienced a culture shock. Many of these small health facilities did not have hot running water. A large cauldron boiled water over an open fire, and medical staff washed their hands by holding them under a faucet as workers kept the ceramic container above the faucet filled. At the same time, two Russian cosmonauts were orbiting the earth in the space station. It was hard to reconcile these extraordinary space events with the poverty and limited resources I observed.

AFRICA

The first quarter of 1997 was my last quarter as a World Bank staff member. My retirement date was March 31, 1997. I only made one more trip, but it was a momentous one. The World Bank would select countries and send a mission to assess its performance, asking: How are we doing? I was fortunate to be included in a multi-sectoral team to visit three African countries and to assess how well the World Bank was performing in developing the health sector and improving the health status of the population. The countries selected were Zambia and Tanzania in the east and Guinea in the west. I had always dreamed of visiting South Africa, and specifically Cape Town, where Afrikaans was still widely in use. As part of my Germanic language studies in college I had read Afrikaans literature, a language that is close to Dutch because the Dutch occupied parts of South Africa during the seventeenth, eighteenth, and nineteenth centuries. They were defeated by the British during the Second Boer War in 1902.

Taking annual leave, I left on Saturday afternoon January 11, ten days before the start of the WB mission on January 20 in Zambia and arrived in Cape Town Sunday evening, staying at the Portswood Hotel. On Monday I went to the Cape Point and the nearby Cape of Good Hope, which is a rocky headland on the Atlantic coast of the Cape Peninsula. The Cape of Good Hope is the dividing point between the Atlantic and Indian Oceans. The meeting of the currents produces dangerous tides and currents, and these troubled seas have witnessed countless maritime disasters in the centuries when ships sailed around the African continent.

The Cape of Good Hope, where the Atlantic meets the Indian Ocean. (PHOTO BY DIEGO DELSO, DELSO.PHOTO, LICENSE CC BY-SA.)

On Tuesday I visited Cape Town, met with, and interviewed a hospital manager to understand better the South African health system, and embarked on a sunset cruise in the evening. I had wanted to take the cable car to the top of the famous Tafelberg, or Table Mountain, that dominates Cape Town, but unfortunately there was no cable service that day.

On Wednesday morning, I left early to arrive in Victoria Falls at noon, staying at the Victoria Falls Safari Lodge. This award-winning lodge is situated on a plateau just four kilometers (2.5 miles) from the majestic Victoria Falls in Zimbabwe. Barstools in the bar are turned toward a wildlife-rich waterhole about two hundred feet away. Sipping a cocktail, one could spot impalas, waterbucks, and warthogs lessening their thirst, especially in late afternoon. Monkeys are all over, and we had to keep the doors to the room balcony closed as they are wont to steal items. The staff joked that they train the monkeys to steal, but the monkeys do enter the rooms and are not afraid of humans.

In the afternoon I visited the famous Victoria Falls on the Zambezi River at the border of Zambia and Zimbabwe. Victoria Falls is classified as the largest waterfall (though not the highest nor widest), based on its combined width of 1,708 meters (5,604 feet) and height of 108 meters (354 feet), resulting in the world's largest sheet of falling water. In height and width Victoria Falls is rivaled only by Argentina and Brazil's Iguazu Falls.

On Thursday I joined a group for a one-day white-water rafting trip down the Zambezi River. Zambezi white-water rafting has been classified by the British Canoe Union as Grade 5—which is "extremely difficult, with twenty-five long and violent rapids, steep gradients, big drops, and pressure areas." A bus took the group to the starting point. The first hour instructed us on how to right the rubber boat in case it turned over. Here I am, almost sixty-five years old—and of course the oldest in the group—rafting down a wild river and hanging on for dear life to a rubber boat with five other men. We stopped for lunch and to rest our muscles halfway through the run. The worst part came at the end, when we had to climb the steep path out of the gorge—a 750-foot climb, which generally takes about twenty minutes. I huffed and puffed my way up the steepness of the gorge in the high humidity. Boys ran past us carrying the deflated rubber boats back to the bus for the next day's excursion. A bit crazy, but a great experience.

On Friday, a twenty-five-minute helicopter ride showed me the full breadth of Victoria Falls through canyons and over rapids, the islands, and neighboring rain forests. It also offered an opportunity to spot wildlife from the sky, even a herd of elephants.

My very first safari excursion was on Saturday, in the Hwange

National Park, which is the largest natural reserve in Zimbabwe. The park hosts more than one hundred mammal and four hundred bird species, with possible spotting of buffalos, zebras, giraffes, elephants, impalas, warthogs, wildebeests, hippos, guinea fowls, and saddle-billed storks. Another most memorable day.

Air Zimbabwe flew me on Sunday afternoon to the capital, Harare, to stay overnight at the Sheraton and continue in the morning to Lusaka, the capital of Zambia, where I met the WB team at the InterContinental Hotel, ending my ten days of South African tourism.

The objective of the WB mission was to assess the performance of health projects in the three countries we were assigned to. We achieved that objective by (a) meeting with and interviewing a wide range of stakeholders (government officials, representatives of bilateral agencies active in these countries, and staff of nongovernmental organizations) inquiring about what the WB was doing right or wrong; and (b) in my case, visiting hospitals, health centers, and health posts, and talking with the health workers.

The first four days were spent in Zambia. The team then flew on Air Tanzania to Dar es Salaam, the seat of most government administration in Tanzania (and its former capital), where we stayed for five days, repeating the program we had followed in Zambia. I had intended to take the hydrofoil to visit the island of Zanzibar, but when I went to the departure area, I was hustled by so many young men to lead me to their preferred company that I got worried and fed up and turned back.

From Tanzania the team flew to Nairobi, the capital of Kenya, staying one night at the Norfolk Hotel, before continuing the next day to West Africa. Our flight on Ethiopian Airlines was scheduled to depart in the afternoon, and two of us took advantage of the free morning to hire a car and a guide to take us on a safari in Nairobi National Park located approximately seven kilometers (four miles) south of Nairobi, where an electric fence separates the park's wildlife from the metropolis. The park boasts a large and varied wildlife population; we saw rhinos, buffalos, jackals, impalas, gnus, giraffes, ostriches, zebras, wildebeests, crocodiles, an eagle, a stork, and yes, we did see a lion pointed out by the guide.

The flight to the west coast made a stop in Lagos, Nigeria, and landed in Abidjan, the capital of the Ivory Coast, in the evening—a seven-hour trip—where we stayed overnight at the InterContinental Hotel. The Air Afrique flight to Guinea, our destination, was scheduled to leave at 4:30 p.m. and arrive in Conakry at 6:25 p.m. At the airport we were informed that the flight had been delayed and rescheduled to leave at 11:00 p.m. Having checked out of the hotel and no desire to sit for six hours in the airport, we took a taxi to the World Bank offices and worked on our back-to-office reports. We finally took off close to midnight and checked in to our hotel in Conakry at about 2:00 a.m. The Palm Camayenne Hotel is set beside the sea and is one of Conakry's best kmown hotels. The team stayed five days in Guinea. The official visits to three African countries had become a five-week trip with stops in a total of seven African countries: South Africa, Zimbabwe, Zambia, Tanzania, Kenya, Ivory Coast, and Guinea.

Professionally, during my visits to rural health facilities, I was struck by the large number of patients admitted for malaria treatment. The presenting complaints noted in the logbooks were, in most cases, high fever, chills, and sweating. We walked through large patient rooms and saw patients hooked to IV infusions of quinine. Malaria was a major killer and still is. HIV/AIDS was already epidemic, but stigma and discrimination hid it from our view, and I did not see any cases. My report therefore highlighted the mortality and morbidity caused by malaria, and it was only a few years later that HIV/AIDS was recognized as a worldwide pandemic still prevalent today.

3 WORLD BANK SPONSORED CONTINUING EDUCATION: CANADA, UK, AND ISRAEL

CANADA

The International Society for Quality in Health Care (ISQua) is a member-based, not-for-profit community dedicated to promoting quality improvement in health care. Each year it holds an international conference. Given my research and publications on the quality of health care I attended two of its annual conferences: the first one in St. John's, Newfoundland, in June 1995, and the second one in Israel in 1996. St. John's is the province's capital and largest city. It is on the island of Newfoundland and is North America's easternmost city and oldest European settlement. Its main export used to be its cod fishery industry but now the city is the center of the oil and gas industry in Eastern Canada. One can see small icebergs drifting in the sea. The city has the largest number of icebreaker ships.

LONDON

The WB financed a five-week training program in family planning and reproductive health at the London School of Hygiene & Tropical Medicine. My academic and experiential background was light on population and family planning issues at a time when population had become front and center in global development programs, and reproductive health projects were heavily promoted by USAID. It was a rainy month of July, but spending five weeks in London was an amazing experience. I took the bus to class and enjoyed being a student again. The academic sessions and homework assignments were complemented by attending plays and events at the National Theatre and at Royal Albert Hall, a visit to Oxford University, and a school trip on a canal boat.

ISRAEL

The last week of May 1996 I traveled to Israel to attend my second five-day annual conference of ISQua in Jerusalem. The check-in area for the Israeli airline El Al at the Brussels Airport was in a separate, closed-in room with the entrance guarded by two policemen. Before going to the check-in counter, I was submitted to an extreme security procedure, including not only the luggage and body check but also an extensive interview.

Why are you going to Israel?

To attend a conference.

Where will you be staying?

At the King David Hotel.

Do you have a reservation?

Yes.

Can you show it? Staying how long?

Five days.

What conference? Can you show me an invitation?

What is your role at the conference?

Can I see a copy of your presentation?

This questioning continued for quite a while. What caused suspicion was the Tunisia visa in my passport. That required a long explanation as why I had visited Tunisia. After about twenty minutes of being grilled, I was allowed to check in, already with a bitter taste in my mouth. The passport control upon arrival at the airport in Tel Aviv generated another long series of questions. I drove from Tel Aviv to Jerusalem along a beautiful highway. The ancient city of Jerusalem is surrounded by walls with entry gates. Upon approaching the gate, I noticed two armed soldiers on top of the gate. Unfortunately, I experienced an emotional déjà vu of armed German soldiers occupying my native village.

With my Catholic upbringing, I wanted to visit Bethlehem in the central West Bank, Palestine, about six miles south of Jerusalem. I could do it on a free Saturday; however, Saturday is the Jewish Sabbath—a day of rest and worship—and Jewish taxi drivers cannot work. So, I took a taxi driven by an Israeli Muslim, who could take me only as far as the checkpoint that separates Israel from the West Bank. After passport control, I took a taxi to continue my six-mile trip to the Manger Square and the Church of the Nativity in Bethlehem. Through a small and low door, I entered the cave called the Nativity Grotto where Jesus is believed to have been born. I said my prayers gratefully for having been able to fulfill this dream. It was already noon by then and I lunched at an Arab restaurant.

The challenge now was to return to the hotel in Jerusalem. A taxi took me back to the checkpoint, and passport control permitted me to enter Israel. No waiting taxis though! A minibus was loading local people, and I was able to squeeze in and pay the fare to Jerusalem. The six-mile round trip had proven to be quite an adventure.

Back at the hotel I went to the restaurant for dinner. This being the Sabbath, the kitchen was closed and there was no warm food, only cold plates prepared the day before. The waiters could not give you a bill or accept a payment. However, at the exit a lady (Muslim?) charged the expense to my room. Passing through the lobby, I noticed that the cashier area was shielded from view by folding screens. This did not mean that you would not be able to pay your bill if you checked out, but that the monetary transactions were hidden from public view.

Exiting the country was almost as difficult as entering it, with long lines and extensive questioning at passport control. At the airport cafeteria I had left my backpack on my chair while selecting food and keeping an eye on my chair. I was immediately approached by security asking me if that was my backpack—any unattended personal belonging is a potential bomb threat. I collected my backpack and went back to the food line.

In sum, I'm pleased I was able to visit Israel, but I have no desire to return.

4 REPRESENTING THE WORLD BANK AT INTERNATIONAL GLOBAL HEALTH EVENTS

My promotion from senior health specialist to lead health specialist solidified my professional standing in the health sector at the World Bank. This resulted in being allowed to accept invitations to make presentations, participate in panel discussions, attend international congresses and meetings, represent the World Bank at international conferences, be a guest lecturer, and in general deepen my knowledge of health sector issues in developing countries. Highlights of the years 1990–1997 include the following.

CHILE

The University of Chile in Santiago invited me to lecture in August 1990. As it was winter in the Southern Hemisphere, I went skiing for one week in Portillo in the Andes Mountains, which is 160 kilometers (100 miles) by vehicle from Santiago. It sits at an elevation of 2,880 meters (9,450 feet) above sea level, and the highest lift reaches 3,310 meters (10,860 feet).

I took advantage of another lecture invitation from the university in January 1992 to travel south to Puerto Montt, with a stop in Concepción, the second largest city in Chile. Puerto

Montt is a port city and commune in southern Chile, located in the Los Lagos Region. The city is the hub of one of the largest salmon aquaculture industries in the world. Fresh salmon is flown daily to world markets and frozen salmon is shipped by ocean to all destinations.

COSTA RICA

I made a presentation and participated in a panel discussions at a one-week seminar organized by Elca Rosenberg of the World Bank in August 1992. The theme of the seminar was Public/Private Partnerships in the health sector.

NEW YORK

A two-day trip in September 1992 to attend meetings and discuss cooperation with two United Nations agencies with whom the World Bank cooperated in many countries: UNICEF (United Nations Children Fund) and UNFPA (United Nations Population Fund).

PHILIPPINES

The regional WHO office and the headquarters of the Asian Development Bank (ADB) are in Manila. My work in East Asia required coordinating development aid financed by the WB with health services development projects financed by the ADB. We worked out an agreement to share offices and local staff in Vientiane, Laos, as both organizations were financing similar health projects but in different regions of the country. The WHO office in Manila wanted to stay informed of WB activities in its region. It was always a pleasure to be in the bustling city of Manila, with its many activities, colorful and crowded jeepney rides, restaurants, historic parks, and friendly people.

INDONESIA

The World Federation of Public Health Associations (WFPHA) is an international, nongovernmental organization representing around five million public health professionals worldwide. I attended the annual meeting of the Asia-Pacific Academic Consortium for Public Health—one of WFPHA's member organizations—on the island of Bali in December 1994. This trip provided the opportunity to stop in Jakarta for a few days and visit with WB colleagues assisting the government.

MALAYSIA

In December 1993, on the way back from South Korea, I stopped in Kuala Lumpur, having accepted an invitation from the Ministry of Health to present a paper on how best to manage quality assurance. Two years later, in November 1995, I represented the World Bank at a four-day regional South Asian meeting in Kuching on the theme "Implementing Population Programs: Quality of Reproductive Health Care as the Way Forward." I learned not to shake hands with attending Iranian female delegates.

LONDON

Each year the World Bank hires a cohort of young people through the Young Professionals Program (YPP). This is a highly selective program and competition is keen. Thousands of applications are received each year for forty-five spots. The selection process starts with a first round that eliminates candidates that do not meet eligibility requirements, followed by a second round that assesses technical competency criteria. Usually about two hundred applicants proceed to the interview round, held in regional locations. I joined my division chief James Socknat to participate in the interview process in London in 1995 covering candidates from European and Middle Eastern countries. Applicants are interviewed separately for one hour by each member of the five-person interview team. There were many public health candidates that year. We would interview three candidates in the morning and two in the afternoon. The whole team would meet at the end of the day to share and defend our scores and make a final decision. It was an arduous five-day task, but nonetheless, I liked the experience of interviewing twenty-five young, ambitious people and defending my decision within the group. Aloysius Ordu managed the YPP process that year.

TUNISIA

The World Bank organized a regional health financing policy meeting In Tunis in June 1995 in which I participated as a lecturer and a panel member. A lunch buffet would be set up in the hall outside the meeting rooms. One day the meeting ran late by more than an hour, but the food had been laid out at the usual time in a warm environment. Lunch resulted in an intestinal infection.

AUSTRIA

For more than half a century, the Salzburg Global Seminar has provided an international forum for bringing together women and men committed to making a difference in their professions and societies. The seminars are conducted at Schloss Leopoldskron in Salzburg. I was honored to be invited to be on the faculty of a one-week seminar March 23–30, 1996, on the theme of "Health Care Partnerships: Meeting the Needs of Underserved Communities". The topic of my presentation was "Absolute Poverty and Social Development in Asia and Latin America," based on my research for a Technical Paper published by the World Bank. The seminar was attended by fifty-four fellows representing thirty countries. Seminar activities are conducted in the Schloss Leopoldskron, built between 1736 and 1744 on seventeen acres with a dramatic view of the Austrian Alps. The faculty rooms were also in the castle. It was quite an unforgettable experience. Here I was, a small-town boy, sleeping and having meals served in an old castle, sitting by the fireplace in the evening with quartets playing classical music, and interacting with professionals from all over the world.

RETIREMENT

After fourteen years and seven months, I retired from the World Bank at the age of sixty-five. It had been a wonderful professional experience. Retirement age was officially at 62 years. My division chief James Socknat and my director Daniel Ritchie recommended to the Vice President to extend my retirement age by three years.

On March 31, 1997, the WB organized a retirement party that my daughter attended with three of my grandchildren. My manager and coworkers said nice words about me—my mother would have believed each word.

5 GLOBAL HEALTH WORK POST–WORLD BANK RETIREMENT: 1997–2017

Upon retirement, I continued to work as a consultant for the next twenty years, until 2017, when I turned eighty-five. I started a consulting firm, The InterHealth Institute, LLC, to manage my consultancies, filed the articles of organization and the trade name application on February 27, 1998, and received approval from the State of Maryland on March 18, 1998. An employer identification number had already been assigned by the IRS in September 1997. I registered with the World Bank as a firm on July 21, 1999, and my vendor identification number was assigned on December 15, 1999. From then on, I contracted with the World Bank for consultancies as a firm and not as an individual consultant.

The World Bank's Quality Assurance Program

Prem Garg created the Quality Assurance Group (QAG) in 1996 to assess the quality and performance of its lending portfolio. Prem retired in 2007 and his legacy was capably solidified by Xavier A. Legrain as the new Director. The department also served as a knowledge management and learning review instrument to propose ways to augment the quality of World Bank products. The lending portfolio covered programs and projects in all sectors of the economy including health, nutrition, and population (HNP). Projects to be reviewed were randomly selected from the lending portfolio. I participated in QAG panels as a lead health specialist reviewing the quality at two levels: at the conceptual design stage and its final performance.

The QAG assessment consisted of a panel staffed by a technical subject specialist (health, in my case), an economist, an environmental specialist, a lawyer, and a gender specialist. Panel members would read all project documentation, interview the task team responsible for designing and supervising project implementation, fill out a questionnaire recording its findings, discuss its finding at a full panel meeting, and submit a final quality report, which was shared with the task team members and their managers. Two consulting days were contractually allocated to each panel member for completing the task.

Task team interviews would take place at headquarters when the task team was based in Washington, D.C. Interviews were conducted using video conferencing when task teams were based in the recipient country. Time zone differences had to be considered, so a twelve-hour time difference meant starting the interview at 7:00 a.m. in Washington when it was 7:00 p.m. for the task team. In my case, this meant leaving my home in Middletown, Virginia, at 5:00 a.m. to drive 85 miles to the World Bank in morning traffic. Oftentimes I would leave the night before and stay overnight in my Cabin John house in Maryland, which I still owned and where my son Lieven was still living.

While the QAG review was mandatory, another World Bank quality improvement procedure, called Quality Enhancement Review (QER), was available at the request of managers. The objective was to ensure that the project design proposed was robust and implementable before submitting the Investment request to the Board of Directors for approval. The QER review was a more meaningful and satisfying approach, as it attempted to prevent potential future implementation delays due to project design errors. The QAG review on the other hand diagnosed mistakes already committed and was an important learning and knowledge-generating tool.

I participated actively in these quality assessments, until about 2012, when the QAG department was deactivated, and its responsibilities transferred to the vice presidencies of the six geographic regions.

International Finance Corporation (IFC): Argentina, Mexico

The IFC is a member of the World Bank Group and the International Finance Corporation became operational in 1956 with 12 staff members. The corporation made its inaugural investment in 1957 by making a $2 million (equivalent to $21 million in 2022) loan to a Brazil-based affiliate of Siemens AG. The corporation operates now with a staff of over 3,400 employees, of which half are stationed in field offices across its member nations. It is the largest development institution focusing exclusively on the private sector in developing countries with a presence in more than 100 countries.

Investments in health care are of more recent origin. In 1997, a consulting firm - Taylor Associates - evaluated IFC's opportunities for healthcare investments in about twenty counties. Its favorable recommendations led to the establishment of a Health Care Unit in the Latin and Caribbean Department. Guy Ellena joined the World Bank in 1986 as a health economist and transferred to IFC in July 1997 as its first Senior Health Specialist. IFC hired Elena Bourganskaia in 1998 as a health specialist. The health unit was added to the Education Department and Guy Ellena became the technical manager of the Health and Education Department in April 2000. Dr. Bourganskaia is currently IFC's Vice President of Corporate Support. IFC deepened its involvement in the health sector by sponsoring a conference in their offices in February 2005 on the theme “Investing In Private Healthcare In Emerging Markets” that examined the most challenging trends in the global healthcare marketplace.

IFC has an active portfolio of $3.5 billion in health care or health related companies. According to its website, IFC helps private providers meet the demand for health care. In line with the World Bank Group’s strategy, it supports governments in their goal of reaching Universal Health Coverage by 2030 through stronger primary health care systems and to provide quality, affordable health services to everyone—regardless of their ability to pay.

IFC investments are based on an acceptable debt/equity ratio. Main items to be financed are for profit hospitals, ambulatory surgical centers, diagnostic centers: clinical laboratories and/or imaging centers, and medical office buildings. Financing is provided for construction of facilities and for medical equipment subject to rigorous cost/benefit analyses and a guarantee of a positive rate of return. This requires assured and regular payments for purchased health care services which are usually paid out of pocket or through private health insurance schemes. Not surprising therefore that IFC client countries are mainly middle income countries such as, for instance, Thailand, Indonesia, Vietnam, Turkey, Mexico, Argentina. However, lower income people in these countries do not have the “ability to pay” for services offered as would the large majority of the population in low income countries. In a few instances, private hospitals receive a government subsidy for uncompensated care provided to patients who do not have the ability to pay. For-profit and not-for-profit private hospitals require an excess of revenue over expenses to stay in business. A critical difference is that in one case the excess or profit is paid out to shareholders who benefit from medical care for sick people whereas excess revenue in the other case is reinvested in improving infrastructure or augmenting the quality of patient care.

IFC has been diversifying its health portfolio. In November 2023, IFC partnered with a health tech company based in Dakar, Senegal to digitize and connect health information with the objective of creating an integrated health platform for Africa. Other 2023 investments support the construction of the largest Pharmaceuticals Factory in Côte d'Ivoire and provide up to $25 million to Uzbekistan's leading grocery retailer helping it construct a state-of-the-art 'green' distribution center.

A different investment approach consists of private investors reaching agreements to joint venture with public hospitals. These investments vary in size ranging from leasing or purchasing automated laboratory equipment or MRI imaging equipment, adding a wing or floors to an existing public building for private patient rooms, ambulatory surgery, diagnostic services, or operating theaters. Agreements specify the contributions of each party in kind and in money, their operating responsibilities, and the respective shares of revenue. Such joint public/private ventures obviate the need for lengthy governmental approval procedures and can be implemented quickly. I witnessed this type of private financing in China as mentioned in the next China section.

In July 1997 I was invited by IFC staff member Guy Ellena to assess an investment opportunity in private hospitals in the states of Hermosillo and Chihuahua, Mexico. I partnered with the Mexican firm Qualimed, led by my colleague Enrique Ruelas, to carry out the consultancy. The main investor was a Dallas-based consortium, CIMA, a subsidiary of the International Hospital Corporation. A policy considered under the Mexican presidency of Ernesto Zedillo would allow members of the Mexican Social Security Institute to opt out of the system and transfer their monthly medical insurance contribution to the private sector. This prospect generated a movement to increase the size of the private health sector, hence the interest of investors in private hospitals. Local business leaders interviewed supported the policy, which ultimately was not approved by the government.

Allowing opting out—as happened in Chile—results in younger, healthier, and more educated workers shifting their earmarked monthly medical payroll deductions to private providers. An opting out policy reduces the budget of the already under resourced public institution leaving it to serve the older and sicker members and their families and thus increasing its deficit and its need for larger government subsidies.

For a second IFC consultancy, in March 1998, I joined a team to assess an investment opportunity in a private, doctor-owned, 155-bed hospital in Córdoba, Argentina. The facility was outdated and needed replacement, and their bed occupancy rate, at 53 percent, should have been higher. The most important issue faced by the Hospital Privado de Córdoba, however, was how to increase its profit margin. Deficits were noticed for seven clinical service departments, such as hemodialysis, ICU for children and adults, tissue typing, pneumology, general surgery, and physical therapy. Specific turnaround recommendations were suggested for implementation. The architect on the team was a first-rate professional who had overseen the building of the new IFC headquarters on Pennsylvania Avenue; unfortunately, he had no experience with hospital functions and their idiosyncratic construction requirements. It was embarrassing to have this pointed out to me by the hospital director. During my career at the World Bank, I often observed architects being assigned to any project that included construction, regardless of the type or size of construction. Many architects had been hired during the earlier years when investments in reconstruction was the main objective. As financing shifted to economic and social development in the 1980s and 1990s, many architects were terminated or chose to manage procurement.

CHINA

The Farlim Group is a Malaysian investment company managed and staffed by Chinese but with a Malay *bumiputra* as chairman. The Chinese managers originated from the area of Quanzhou, in the province of Fujian, and still speak its dialect. Farlim was investing in a large development project in Quanzhou, including office buildings, an international hotel, shopping malls, and residential buildings. It was considering adding a private hospital to their investment program. My Malaysian colleague Mohamed Sultan recommended me to Farlim to carry out a financial feasibility study for a Quanzhou international medical center. I submitted a proposal to Farlim that included a team of five Chinese nationals and two expatriates. On the Chinese side there was a senior physician assisted by a midlevel physician, a financial analyst, an architect, and the team leader (Zhou Ji An). The expatriates were the hospital and equipment planner for the functional and space programs (Walther Verniers) and me as the study team leader. To evaluate the financial and technical viability of investing in a private hospital in Quanzhou, the team visited five hospitals, three industries, and interviewed senior doctors, factory managers, and government officials in August 1997. The final report concluded that the concept of building, equipping, and operating a private hospital in Quanzhou was financially, commercially, and technically viable and sustainable.

Bureaucratic procedures and approvals to construct a private hospital were so onerous and time consuming that the hospital was never built. Chinese investors—mainly from Hong Kong—bypassed this bureaucratic bottleneck by adding private wings to existing public hospitals, which could then be presented and accepted as an extension or renovation project and not a new construction. An alternative private investment was to purchase high-end laboratory or imaging equipment, which would then be leased to the public hospital against monthly payments or revenue sharing.

DOMINICAN REPUBLIC

With the decline of horse racing, the government of the Dominican Republic converted in 1996 the centrally located hippodrome into a large medical complex. President Joaquín Balaguer by decree designated this vast area of 221 thousand square feet—naming it Plaza de la Salud—for the construction of the Hospital General de la Plaza de la Salud (HGPS) and the Centers for Diagnostics and Advanced Medicine and Medical Conferences and Telemedicine (CEDIMAT). Construction was financed by the Dominican government. Subsequently, the land occupied by the two hospitals was legally transferred in 2003 to the boards of both HGPS and CEDIMAT.

The presidential decree conferred autonomy to the HGPS as a nonprofit medical institution. It is managed by a board of directors and has the legal status of an NGO. The first fifteen-member board of directors was appointed by the 1996 presidential decree, and replacing retiring or deceased members is the prerogative of the board, which is composed of physicians, businessmen, and individuals dedicated to serving the Dominican community. The board appoints the hospital director, the chief financial officer, the chief nursing officer, and the heads of clinical departments.

The HGPS is an acute-care, 264-bed facility with a bed occupancy rate of 60 percent and an average length of patient stay of four days. Its US$50 million annual budget is financed by patient fees and insurance payments, pharmacy and cafeteria profits, and donations. The government subsidy in 2014 was 8 percent of its operating cost to offset the expense of uncompensated care. Low-income patients receive a discount of up to 40 percent after an evaluation of their socioeconomic status. Medical indigents received free care.

CEDIMAT is a highly specialized, 76-bed cardiovascular nonprofit hospital granted autonomy as an NGO by presidential decree. The statutes that specify its operating procedures were signed by the president in 1999. They include the names of the board president and the board's eighteen members. The board president is the Metropolitan Archbishop of Santo Domingo. The selection of replacements of board members for causes of resignation or death is decided by the board. The director general of the hospital is appointed by a two-thirds vote of the board. The statutes specify in detail the role, functions, and responsibilities of the board and of the director general.

CEDIMAT is a fully autonomous hospital with complete authority to manage all aspects of its operations: staffing, financing, payments, investments, procurement, service provision, and information management. Its main source of revenue is payments by patients and by insurance companies. The hospital receives a subsidy from the government equivalent to 6 percent of its revenue. The subsidy compensates the hospital for the discounts it provides to patients unable to pay the full amount of the cost of the care provided after evaluating their socioeconomic status. The hospital received international accreditation from the Canadian Accreditation Council in 2015.

My consultancy report was the first documentation of the origin and the development of the Plaza de la Salud, its institutional components, its financing, and its legal status. The legal office of the presidency allowed me access to all presidential decrees related to the conversion of the hippodrome into the Plaza de la Salud and the construction and operation of the health facilities on the site.

PAKISTAN

The Department of Health of the government of Punjab was interested in granting autonomy to its public hospitals. I was invited to examine the feasibility of the proposed policy. I traveled to Lahore, the capital of the province of Punjab and the country's second-most populous city after Karachi, the first week of March 1999. I visited four hospitals—the Holy Family Hospital in Rawalpindi, the Jinnah Hospital in Lahore, the Shaikh Zayed Hospital in Rahim Yar Khan, and the Lahore General Hospital—and interviewed government officials and hospital managers. A first draft of a working paper was delivered at the end of March, and I returned to discuss my findings and recommendations on April 18.

At the request of the secretary of health of the province of Punjab (Muhammad I. Qureshi), I also focused on the management of academic health centers. He was quite concerned about the organizational, institutional, and financial arrangements and disruptive interpersonal management issues between medical schools and academic or teaching hospitals. Deans of medical schools managed or attempted to manage the university hospitals. He asked me to prepare and send him a report on how other countries were dealing with this dual authority and responsibility situation. My extensive review documented the options used in the U.S. and the U.K., which—although idiosyncratic—nonetheless provided alternatives for the secretary to consider.

LEBANON

My consulting firm, The InterHealth Institute LLC, submitted a proposal to the Ministry of Public Health of the Republic of Lebanon on July 26, 1999, to conduct an external consultancy on implementing the Law on Autonomy for Public Hospitals. The two-person consultancy team consisted of myself and an international lawyer with experience in reviewing legal frameworks for health sector reforms. In addition to the legal analysis, we collected empirical evidence from field visits to four hospitals and from interviews with public and private sector stakeholders to corroborate our findings. We visited hospitals in the south (Sidon and Tyre) and the north (Tripoli). The Tripoli hospital was constructed under the French mandate in the 1930s and should have been demolished and replaced years earlier. Renovations and additions could not make it a safe and functional health facility. I recall arriving at the hospital and seeing the impressive monumental façade with a steep staircase to reach the entrance. One needed to be quite healthy to climb the steps to be admitted to the hospital. We presented our findings and recommendations to the Ministry of Public Health on November 2, 1999.

At the request of the Ministry of Public Health, we submitted a second proposal in 2000 to assist in carrying out the recommendations made in our 1999 report. A local lawyer (Emile Aoun) was added to the team to assist in analyzing the national laws governing public hospitals to assess the most feasible autonomy options. This time the contract was signed with the government's Council for Development and Reconstruction, and not with the Ministry of Public Health, on March 31, 2000.

The strategic approach required suggestions for establishing new institutional structures and new organizational, financial, and legal relationships to manage public hospitals. We consulted with key stakeholders to get input from those who would approve the institutions being proposed for more autonomy and from those who would manage and use the services of the new entities. Therefore, a participatory approach was used to foster consensus building. We traveled to Beirut in April and June. The draft report in June 2000 was followed by a formal presentation of our recommendations in October and the submission of the final report on November 6, 2000.

It was always a delight to spend time in Beirut. The city had suffered much from the civil war and political unrest but kept rebounding. I enjoyed strolling on the boardwalk in the evening, watching people, buying some sweets, and observing the waves of the Mediterranean Sea. Hotel service and restaurants are of international quality. Restaurants start serving dinner at the late hour of 9:00 p.m.

I visited Byblos, about forty-two kilometers (twenty-six miles) north of Beirut, which is known for its fish restaurants, open-air bars, and outdoor cafés and sipping raki, an unsweetened, often anise-flavored alcoholic drink. Byblos has been continuously inhabited since 5000 BC, making it one of the oldest continuously inhabited cities in the world. There is a legend that the name Byblos is the source of the word "bible" because the bible was originally written on papyrus that was in abundant supply in Byblos. The papyrus plant produces a material like thick paper that was used in ancient times as a writing surface. Beqaa Valley, about twenty miles east of Beirut, is home to Lebanon's famous vineyards and wineries. We drove through the valley to reach the mountain residence of a Lebanese colleague.

Chile and Lebanon share similar features. Geographically, both are long but narrow countries with a long seacoast, valleys, and mountains. Beaches and mountains are within driving distance; vineyards and wineries are plentiful. Seafood is abundant and fresh.

ROMANIA

A 1997 World Bank contract for a health system reform program included fourteen team members, Romanian counterparts, travel, lodging, interpreters, translations, and drivers. The team traveled three times to Bucharest—in January, March, and May 1998—and a final report was delivered on June 5, 1998. I served as task manager and contributed to the quality improvement component. Suzanne McLees provided valuable project management assistance and professional input on the burden of disease component.

The political regime change in Romania in late 1989 had triggered equally momentous changes in the economic and social environments. The government decided to change the health sector from centrally planned and taxation-based financing of health services to a social insurance–based system that would finance services more efficiently and equitably. The social insurance system would be funded by employer/employee contributions augmented by tax-based finances for low-income groups and for national public health programs. Over fifty professionals cooperated under this contract in assisting Romania in the daunting task of charting the course for a historic health sector reform.

The reform program focused on five strategic change areas: the burden of disease and cost-effective interventions; financing health services and paying providers; organization, management, and delivery of health services; physical infrastructure and technological assets; and the health workforce.

The final report included findings, recommendations, and detailed costs of recommendations.

MALAYSIA

The government of Malaysia was considering introducing a national health insurance scheme and signed a contract with a consulting firm from Portland, Maine, to make recommendations on how to prepare for its eventual implementation. The firm's project leader had taken courses from William Hsiao at the Harvard School of Public Health and wanted to hire him as a consultant. Bill Hsiao, an endowed professor, is internationally known for his expertise in health insurance issues and very much in demand. Not comfortable approaching and inviting Bill, the project leader called me, knowing that I had worked with Bill in China and that we were friends. I called Bill and he agreed to join me for a ten-day consultancy.

What linked the people involved in this venture was the University of Minnesota program in Healthcare Administration. The Portland firm was staffed by alumni; Mohamed Sultan, the intermediary in Kuala Lumpur, is an alumnus, and so am I.

During our time in Kuala Lumpur, Bill and I were wined and dined by the country's largest private financial company, which wanted us to recommend that the collection and distribution of medical insurance fees be managed by their firm. This would privatize the financial management of the national medical insurance program. Neither Bill nor I were ideologically and pragmatically in tune with this privatization approach. We had fruitful meetings with government officials and made a set of robust recommendations.

ECUADOR

The World Bank financed a $45 million health services project in 1998 to assist in modernizing health services delivery. The task team leader was Patricio Marquez, who invited me to be part of the team and be responsible for the hospital modernization component. The team traveled to Ecuador in July 1999, visiting Guayaquil, Cuenca, Tena, and Quito. Subsequently, I signed a one-year consultancy contract with the Ministry of Public Health on providing more autonomy to public hospitals. The contract specified a monthly stipend and four visits to the country. The first two-week visit took place November/December 1999, followed by a second two-week visit in March 2000. Two pilot hospitals were selected: the Enrique Garces Hospital in the south of Quito and the Vicente Corral Moscoso Hospital in Cuenca. I also visited two private hospitals in Quito: The Hospital Metropolitano and the cancer hospital SOLCA. The report at the end of the second visit included a set of recommendations with options that benefited from my experience in Lebanon.

Progress made during the first two visits slowed down due to a change in the leadership at the ministry. The president appointed a well-known and highly respected hospital clinician with limited management skills and no knowledge of public health issues. Initially, moving the public hospital sector toward a greater degree of autonomous decision-making remained a priority, as the pilot project was expanded by adding two more public hospitals: the Eugenio Espejo Hospital in Quito and one hospital in Guayaquil. Ultimately, however, management changes made by the new leadership resulted in discontinuing implementing the rest of the signed contract.

KINGDOM OF SAUDI ARABIA

In 1996, as a staff member of the World Bank, I had participated in a conference in Riyadh organized by Dr. Mohammed Hassan Mufti, director general of the Security Forces Hospital. Subsequently, Dr. Mufti invited me in 1998 to make a presentation at the Symposium on Health Sector Development and Reform. Now that I was retired from the World Bank, Dr. Mufti and I discussed joining forces to create the first Saudi health care consulting company. We signed a memorandum of understanding and created Al-Mashura Healthcare Consulting as the first in Saudi

Arabia, with offices in Riyadh and Washington, D.C., with Dr. Mufti as president and me as executive vice president. Al-Mashura Healthcare Consulting offered services to providers, payers, and purchasers of health care services to improve patient access and quality of care, while identifying/implementing cost-effective practices for effective use of resources. We rented office space, developed brochures and marketing materials, and hired a Lebanese man as a manager and business promoter. To prepare jump-start this partnership, I flew to Riyadh in October and December 1998 and in May and October 1999.

In 2000, Kluwer Academic Publishers of New York published a book written by Dr. Mufti: *Healthcare Development Strategies in the Kingdom of Saudi Arabia*. I had prepared the data and formatted the tables for his analysis and insights. My former World Bank administrative assistant handled the typing and formatting with advice from the publisher.

The working relationship between Dr. Mufti and me developed into a close friendship. On several occasions I was invited to his home, and once I had dinner with the whole family: his wife, who was a school principal, and his four children. The family followed the daily Muslim prayer schedule, with the men standing in front and the wife and daughters behind them. I could not participate, of course, but respected their faith. His status as director general of a prestigious hospital that took care of the country's security forces and being a physician to the royal family provided him with resources, authority, and respect. Dr. Mufti always had his staff take of my travel arrangements. I would fly first class on Saudia, the Saudi Arabian airline, from Dulles International Airport to Riyadh. Security was strict upon departure, and a second security check was done before entering the plane.

In October 2001, Al-Mashura signed a consulting contract with the Islamic Development Bank (IsDB), headquartered in Jeddah. The contract was to carry out a "Study of the Medical Benefits System for IsDB's Staff." The IsDB is a regional development bank* established in July 1975 that promotes social and economic development in fifty-seven Muslim countries. We initiated the study with a two-week visit to the headquarters in Jeddah. The study team consisted of Dr. Mufti, me, Hisham Fakha, and Mintu Pal. Mintu was an actuarial analyst responsible for calculating the actuarial cost of current and projected medical benefits for the 861 active staff, dependents, and retirees. A copy of the final report was delivered on March 4, 2002, along with a PowerPoint presentation of the highlights.

Jeddah is a more attractive city than Riyadh to visit or work in. It is the largest seaport on the Red Sea, with a population of about four million, and is Saudi Arabia's commercial capital. It features a long walkway along the Red Sea decorated with open-air sculptures and works of art. The Riyadh I recall consisted of government buildings, office towers, shopping malls, hotels, and walled-in residences. One does not walk outside in Riyadh in the summer months at over 100 degrees Fahrenheit.

A few years later Dr. Mufti was diagnosed with a cancer that metastasized quickly. He was flown to Boston for treatment accompanied by his family. The Saudi government paid for his treatment and for the lodging arrangements for his wife and children. He called me from the hospital detailing clinically what was happening to him but essentially saying goodbye. I lost a close friend and business partner. The Al-Mashura company still has a website, but I do not know if it is still active.

MEXICO

Oaxaca is one of thirty-one Mexican states, located in southeastern Mexico. It is bordered by the states of Guerrero, Puebla, Veracruz, and Chiapas and has a significant coastline on the Pacific Ocean. The highest elevation is 3,720 meters (12,200 feet). The state, with its four million people, is best known for its

* Other regional development banks are the Inter-American Bank, the Asian Development Bank, and the Africa Development Bank.

indigenous peoples and cultures. The most numerous and best known are the Zapotecs and the Mixtecs, but there are sixteen peoples that are officially recognized. Tourist attractions include archeological sites such as Monte Albán and Mitla and its various native cultures and crafts. The coast has sandy beaches in Puerto Escondido and Puerto Ángel. Oaxaca is also one of the most biologically diverse states in Mexico, ranking in the top three along with Chiapas and Veracruz for numbers of reptiles, amphibians, mammals, and plants.

The purpose of my consultancy was to assist in implementing a rural health project. I arrived a day late in the state's capital, Oaxaca de Juárez, because heavy rains had flooded the airport runways in Mexico City canceling all flights. The consultancy required visits to health clinics and health posts and interviews with health professionals and patients. The diverse indigenous cultures and their acceptance of modern medicine presented challenging problems. I had lived in Mexico for four years but still was not quite prepared for the range of languages, customs, dresses, musical instruments, and variety of food in one small geographic area. Definitely an educational health project visit.

DOMINICAN REPUBLIC

The loan for the Dominican Republic Health Reform Support Program in the amount of US$30 million was approved in June 2003. The team leader Patricio Marquez asked me to assist in preparing the documentation and justification for this four-year operation, helping to shepherd it through the Dominican and World Bank bureaucracy, and to provide technical assistance in its implementation. The project would support the preparation, validation, and dissemination of supplementary norms and regulations to the General Health Law and the Social Security Law, with an emphasis on configuring regional health networks.

The regional hospital Jaime Mota in the province of Barahona was the pilot hospital for regionalizing a health network using provinces as a basic organizing unit, and the team worked intensively with this hospital. This project required many trips to Santo Domingo and by car to the province of Barahona. It was very satisfying to develop close working relationships with national counterparts, to develop friendships, and to increase an understanding of the cultures of the health system and of the country.

EL SALVADOR

On January 13 and February 13, 2001, El Salvador was rocked by two powerful earthquakes followed by thousands of strong aftershocks. The first quake, measuring 7.6 on the Richter scale, occurred off the southern Pacific coast and was felt from Mexico to Panama. It was the strongest earthquake in El Salvador since the 1915 quake. The second quake, although lower in magnitude (6.6), was centered about 30 km southeast of San Salvador, causing further damage. The total amount of damage and loss from the January 13, 2001, earthquake was estimated at US$1,255.4 million.

The health care sector suffered extensive damage. Altogether, 113 of the 361 MOH health facilities were affected, including 23 of 30 national hospitals, 82 health centers, and numerous other structures including departmental offices, labs, etc. Six of the largest hospitals sustained important damage. The more damaged hospitals continued to operate under large tents, in trailers, and in other provisional structures while others reduced operations. Damaged health facilities accounted for 55 percent of health care services delivery capacity.

The World Bank responded with a fast-paced lending operation that took less than six months between the June project identification mission and Board approval of an emergency loan in December. A ten-day project design mission July 11-20 was led by Gerard La Forgia and Sandra Rosenhouse as co-Task Team Leaders and I participated as a consultant. Agreement was reached with the government to rehabilitate six large hospitals, viz. San Juan de Dios in San Miguel, San Rafael in La Libertad, Santa Teresa in Zacatecoluca, San Pedro in Usulután, Santa Gertrudis in San Vicente, and Maternidad Nacional in San Salvador.

Appraisal of the design and cost of the "El Salvador Emergency Reconstruction and Health Services Extension Project" was completed during a working visit from September 24 to October 3, 2001. This mission was led by Sandra Rosenhouse and myself as co-task managers and my responsibility was specifically to oversee all activities associated with the hospital infrastructure component. An earthquake emergency reconstruction and health services extension project loan in the amount of US$142.6 million was approved by the Board of Directors on December 4, 2001.

HIV/AIDS Pandemic with a Focus on the Caribbean Countries

Acquired immune deficiency syndrome (AIDS) was first recognized by the United States Centers for Disease Control and Prevention (CDC) in 1981 and its cause—the human immunodeficiency virus (HIV) infection—was identified in 1983.Since the start of the epidemic until 2022, 85.6 million people have been infected with HIV, and the disease has caused an estimated 40.4 million deaths worldwide. HIV/AIDS is considered a pandemic—a disease outbreak which is present over a large area and is actively spreading. World Bank lending for AIDS in Africa averaged only $18 million per year from 1988 to 1999. It was only in 1999 and 2000 that the World Bank and other international donors realized the potential devastation being caused by the HIV/AIDS pandemic. Subsequently, the number of HIV projects financed and implemented by the World Bank increased substantially, and cumulative investments for HIV since 1989 have totaled $4.6 billion. The World Bank's Multi-Country AIDS Program was the first $1 billion commitment to the global AIDS response.

The Caribbean region had the second highest HIV prevalence rate after sub-Saharan Africa. A red cover seminal report was prepared by the World Bank in 2000. The Task team leader was Patricio V. Marquez, Lead Health Specialist, Charles Griffin was the HNP Sector Manager and Evangeline Javier was the HNP Director for the LAC region. This report provided an overview of the challenges and opportunities in addressing the problem of HIV/AIDS in the Caribbean, presented a snapshot of the HIV/AIDS epidemic in the region, and identified the potential role of the World Bank. The report was presented during the Meeting of the Caribbean Group on Cooperation in Economic Development (CGCED), held at the World Bank June 12-16, 2000. This meeting involved Prime Ministers, Ministers of Finance, and other key decision-makers from member countries, as well as senior representatives of other international organizations. The report was further disseminated during the Regional Conference on HIV/AIDS held in Barbados, September 11-12, 2000.

Countries with the highest rates are Haiti, Trinidad and Tobago, Bahamas, Guyana, and Belize. HIV transmission in the Caribbean is occurring largely through heterosexual intercourse. The region is heterogeneous in terms of its political, economic, cultural, ethnic, religious, and linguistic characteristics, which present complex challenges in the response to AIDS. The region has many languages—Spanish (spoken by more than 60 percent of the population but only in Cuba and the Dominican Republic), French (20 percent), and English (16 percent), with the remaining speaking Dutch and Creole.

Population size varies from smaller island states such as Anguilla with 8,000, Haiti with 8 million and Cuba with 11 million inhabitants. The majority of the population is of African descent. The region has also people of European and Asian ancestry, as well as indigenous populations such as Carib, Arawak, Garifuna, and Taino peoples. The Caribbean peoples are also from diverse religious backgrounds—Christian, Hindu, Muslim, and others.

Between 2002 and 2012 I was actively engaged in designing HIV/AIDS projects, monitoring their implementation, and providing technical assistance in the Caribbean countries of Guyana, Saint Lucia, Saint Vincent and the Grenadines, Saint Kitts and Nevis, Jamaica, Grenada, Trinidad and Tobago, Barbados, Belize, and the Dominican Republic. Patricio Marquez initiated the first two projects and Mary Mulusa continued efficiently designing and managing all other projects. In 2005 I was a team member with staff from five international organizations that carried out a review of the HIV/AIDS program in nine countries that had World Bank–financed projects. The twelve-person review team represented the British Department for International Development (Heather Royes, Rosemary Barber-Madden); the Global Fund to Fight AIDS, Tuberculosis, and Malaria (Wolfgang Munar, Jessie Schutt-Aine); WHO/PAHO (Regine Meyer); the Joint United Nations Program on HIV/AIDS (Miriam Maluwa, Kristin Shutz); and the World Bank (Elizabeth Mziray, Nadeem Mohammad, Ahmadou M. Ndiaye, me). The team leader was Daniel Ritchie.

Each Caribbean country has its own identity and idiosyncrasies. Belize still has an indigenous Garifuna population. Guyana and Trinidad and Tobago are the only two Caribbean countries with a population evenly split between people of African and of Indian descent, and electoral votes follow ethnic lines. The small Grenadines are the sister islands of Saint Vincent and are a haven for sailboats and celebrities. Saint Lucia is the second most popular wedding destination for British couples. Oil revenue makes Trinidad economically more prosperous. Guyana is geographically located in South America but faces and interacts with the Caribbean, while its southern region is a rain forest bordering Brazil. Jamaica is the only island that sits right in the middle of the Caribbean Sea, while other islands have a Caribbean Sea side and an Atlantic Ocean side.

Traveling throughout the region is mainly island hopping in small propeller airplanes on LIAT and Caribbean Airlines. Antigua is a major hub for changing planes. Caribbean people are highly mobile and may live on one island and work on another. Marriages between couples from different islands are common. Higher education institutions are mainly located in Jamaica, Trinidad, Dominican Republic, Barbados, and Guyana.

• • •

The following are highlights from my ten years traveling and working in the Caribbean:

GUYANA

The team (me, Shiyan Chao, Carmen Carpio) took a three-day trip to visit the Iwokrama Forest, a tropical forest in central Guyana close to the Brazil border. We flew in an eight-person propeller plane from Guyana's capital, Georgetown, to Annai, and then took a minibus to the Iwokrama Forest. The road links the capital with Brazil yet is poorly maintained. On the way we stopped on a small bridge to see parts of an anaconda hiding by a river—from a respectable distance. Excursions on the river Essequibo revealed a dramatic view of birds, reptiles, mammals, and fish. Apparently, we were very lucky to see a harpy eagle, and our pictures convinced the other guides at the camp that we indeed saw one. More common birds were the toucan, the red-and-green macaw, the blue-headed parrot, the great white egret, the ibis, the pied plover, and the kingfisher. Our guide also pointed out green iguanas, a black spider monkey, and a red howler monkey in the trees. The river contained caimans and a fish called the arapaima, which is an air breather and the largest freshwater scaled fish in the world. The canopy walkway on the

A very rare harpy eagle in the Iwokrama Forest, in central Guyana, one of the last pristine tropical forests left.

return drive allowed us to look down on the trees instead of up. It was an unforgettable three-day experience.

SAINT LUCIA

This island is memorable for its pair of dramatically tapered mountains (the Pitons), its sulfur mines and baths, its waterfalls, the arrival of huge cruise ships dwarfing its capital, Castries, and Marigot Bay, with its charming harbor featured in the 1967 film *Doctor Doolittle*, also popular for its resorts, restaurants, and kayaking spots.

GRENADINES

The Grenadines in the Lesser Antilles are islands in the nation of Saint Vincent and the Grenadines. They are known for yacht-filled harbors and sailing spots like the reef-lined island of Bequia, with secluded Princess Margaret Beach. Mustique is a private island with luxury villas and quiet beaches. We flew in a small aircraft over the blue, shallow waters of the islands, landed and lunched in Bequia, and visited a small health post that justified the ministry's expense of our excursion. The main island has a desalinization plant, as potable water is a scarce resource.

SAINT KITTS AND NEVIS

Saint Kitts, also known more formally as Saint Christopher Island, and the neighboring island of Nevis constitute the country of Saint Kitts and Nevis. The west side of the island borders the Caribbean Sea, and the eastern coast faces the Atlantic Ocean. Saint Kitts and Nevis are separated by a shallow three-kilometer (two-mile) channel. Saint Kitts has a population of around 40,000 and Nevis has about 9,000 inhabitants (and would like to become an independent country!). Nevis attracts more tourism, with its resorts on old plantations and its relaxing atmosphere. I visited the hospital in Nevis and stayed for a long, relaxing weekend. Eight of the nine physicians in the Nevis hospital were from other countries, and they view their stay in Nevis as a stepping stone to eventually emigrate to the United States.

JAMAICA

The University of the West Indies is the largest and oldest higher education provider in the Commonwealth Caribbean, with campuses in Mona, Jamaica; Saint Augustine, Trinidad and Tobago; Cave Hill, Barbados; and an Open Campus serving sixteen Caribbean island-nations. As a World Bank team, we visited the Mona campus to explore potential research collaboration. The 2019 *Times Higher Education* World University Rankings places it in the top 5 percent of universities globally.

GRENADA

We worked with Grenada, providing technical assistance to a complex HIV/AIDS project with execution authority divided across three ministries. This complex design required several trips. The capital, St. George's, was built by the Spaniards on a hilltop with steep and narrow streets. The team stayed at a beachfront hotel and enjoyed several good seafood restaurants.

I was fascinated by the history of Grenada,* with the invasion by American troops during the Reagan administration in 1983. The Prime Minister Maurice Bishop cooperated with Cuba and the USSR on various trade and foreign policy issues, but he sought to maintain a "non-aligned" status. Hardline Marxist party members deemed Bishop insufficiently revolutionary, and Bishop was executed together with seven of his cabinet members. The location of their remains is still a mystery today. The overthrow of a moderate government by one which was strongly pro-communist gave the administration of President Reagan the excuse it was looking for to justify an invasion six days later. Reagan also claimed that particularly worrying was the presence of Cuban construction workers and military personnel who were building a 3,000-meter (10,000-foot) airstrip in Grenada. U.S. troops ousted the government and took full control of the country within three days and withdrew from Grenada in December 1983. Reagan claimed that Cuba—under the direction of the Soviet Union—would use Grenada as a refueling stop for Cuban and Soviet airplanes loaded with weapons destined for Central American communist insurgents, even though Cuba is about 966 kilometers (600 miles) from Central America and Grenada is over a thousand miles from Central America! Clearly a paranoiac overreach.

Grenada, with a population of about 125,438 in 2022, is home to St. George's University, a private international university, offering degrees in medicine, veterinary medicine, public health,

---

* The U.S. has supported regime change militarily or through covert CIA operations in many Latin American countries, usually in support of right-wing forces or right-wing authoritarian governments: Guatemala 1954, Dominican Republic 1961, Brazil 1964, Chile 1973, Uruguay 1973, Argentina 1976, Panama 1989, El Salvador, and Nicaragua civil wars. The *Washington Post* (December 23, 2016) reports that between 1947 and 1989, the United States tried to change other nations' governments seventy-two times. That worldwide statistic includes sixty-six covert operations and six overt ones.

nursing, arts and sciences, and business. Some of its approximately 5,000 students are from Grenada, but the vast majority of students are from other countries. Many medical students are U.S. citizens who study in Grenada and return to the U.S. to complete their medical training and to practice.

The Russian Federation

The World Bank's Country Assistance Strategy in the Russian Federation for 2003 to 2005 included preparation of a report examining policy and program options relevant to the health challenges in the country. Patricio Marquez invited me as a team member and I traveled to Moscow three times to assist in preparing the report: December 2004, June 2005, and December 2005.

President Vladimir Putin, in his annual address to the Federal Assembly of the Russian Federation in May 2004, criticized the failure of the health care reform to produce significant results, as evidenced by Russia's lagging behind many countries in key health indicators. Life expectancy in Russia, he noted, is twelve years less than life expectancy in the United States, eight years less than in Poland, and five years less than in China—a situation the president attributed to "the high death rate in the working-age population." Russian adults die prematurely and suffer from illnesses that, to a large extent, are avoidable or treatable. In 2001 the average life expectancy at birth among males in Russia was fifty-nine years—or about fifteen years less than the average life expectancy in other Group of Eight (G-8) countries.

Non-communicable diseases and traffic injuries represent the bulk of morbidity, disability, and premature death. Three risk factors—high blood pressure, high cholesterol, and tobacco—are estimated to contribute to more than 75 percent of Russia's deaths.

Russia is the first developed country in the history of modern nations to experience a peacetime loss in life expectancy. Declining birth rates and high mortality rates were expected to continue to reduce sharply the total population of Russia, which numbered approximately 142 million.

The final WB report focusing on adult health and aptly titled "Dying Too Young" was well received and became a wake-up call to reform the health system. This was one of the most exciting analytic projects I participated in during my career. Staying in Moscow is not a hardship either. The team stayed at the Marriott, the Hyatt, and the Kempinski hotels, consecutively. The World Bank offices are comfortable, well equipped, and have a well-managed, quality professional staff. The World Bank country director for the Russian Federation at that time was Kristalina Georgieva, a Bulgarian national, who served as acting president of the World Bank in 2019 and is now the managing director of the International Monetary Fund.

My last two-week trip to Russia took place in April 2007 as a member of a mission to identify a possible health service restructuring project in the Chuvash Republic, with a rest stop at the Hyatt in Moscow. The government of the Chuvash Republic and the Word Bank team agreed on a health policy and an action plan that would reduce premature mortality and preventable morbidity and disabilities of the working-age population resulting from the high incidence of non-communicable diseases and road traffic injuries.

Traveling to the Chuvash Republic always meant an overnight journey from Moscow that takes approximately fourteen hours each way. The "express train" left Moscow at 7:00 p.m. and arrived in the capital of Chuvashia (Cheboksary) at 9:00 a.m. We were allowed to travel first class, meaning two people in a sleeping compartment, and were given a prepackaged meal. Our Russian colleagues were assigned a compartment for four people.

Working in Moscow or transiting through Moscow on the way

to Chuvashia or Voronezh provided the opportunity to attend performances at the Bolshoi Theatre. Buying tickets at the box office on short notice was never possible, as shows were always sold out, but this inconvenience was easily solved by purchasing tickets from the hotel concierge at an inflated price. I do not remember how many Bolshoi performances I have seen, but I do recall vividly two performances: One is *Don Quixote*, based on the novel by Miguel de Cervantes, where Don Quixote enters the stage sitting on his noble white steed, Rocinante, then descends majestically from the horse, which is then led away (his squire, Sancho Panza, did not enter the stage on his donkey!). The second is *The Nutcracker*, where the Sugar Plum Fairy ushers Clara and the prince at the end of the show into an elevator that slowly rises and carries them away as they wave goodbye to all their friends and family.

CAMEROON

The World Bank offered me a consultancy in the Republic of Cameroon for twenty-one days in May and June 2006 to join a team to assist the implementation of the Multi-Sectoral HIV-AIDS National Program. HIV/AIDS was a generalized epidemic in Cameroon, with about 5.5 percent of the population between ages fifteen and forty-nine infected with HIV.

Cameroon has a population of about 24 million and is bilingual, with French and English as official languages (although French is by far the most used language). In 1919, after World War I, Cameroon was split into French Cameroun and British Cameroons. French Cameroun gained independence from France in 1960, and in 1961 the formerly British Southern Cameroons gained independence and joined with French Cameroun to form the Federal Republic of Cameroon. Violence spurred by the linguistic split broke out in 2017, with many in the English-speaking minority supporting secession.

Upon arrival in the capital, Yaoundé, on Air France, I was not allowed in the country for lack of a yellow fever vaccination certificate. The task team leader (Jean J. Delion) had neglected to tell me about this requirement. The choice was to be vaccinated right then and there or return on the next Air France flight. I was quite uneasy about being injected at an airport in Africa; however, I noticed that the physician in charge was using disposable needles, so I agreed to the vaccination, paid US$16, received a certificate, and was allowed to enter the luggage area.

The second mistake on this trip was ordering a salade Niçoise for lunch in a nice restaurant, resulting in a virulent intestinal infection. I was knocked out for two days, ordering only tea and toast from room service. I should have known better by then never to eat uncooked food in a developing country.

Meetings were conducted in French, but the Anglophone Cameroonians would speak English. Participants understood both languages, and nobody ever objected. It was an interesting experience for me, having grown up in a bilingual country where the same linguistic accommodations and acceptance do not prevail.

SENEGAL

I visited Senegal for ten days in August 2007 as a member of a World Bank/UNAIDS Technical Support Team to assess the implementation of the Senegal Multi-Sectoral HIV/AIDS Project. The team led by Aissatou Diack was tasked to review the existing processes, identify implementation bottlenecks, and recommend pragmatic actions for a more efficient project implementation. My responsibility was to review the institutional and implementation arrangements.

I noticed the project's high operating cost of close to half a million dollars per year. The World Bank had recommended outsourcing the fiduciary functions of the project to a private firm, as some economists strongly believed in the greater efficiency of the private sector. I noticed that the contract with the private accounting firm included five days of consulting each month by the owner of the firm at a daily rate of US$800. Coincidentally the private owner and the WB project coordinator who had signed the contract had been classmates. Corruption is often an integral part of a local culture and occurs in both public- and private-sector interactions.

Senegal is a Francophone Muslim country, where about half of all marriages are polygamous. When visiting a rural health center, I reviewed the patient data collection form to understand the kind of medical data being collected. For the first time in my career, I noticed that women were asked if they were the first or the second wife in their marriage. I did not understand fully the health implications of a polygamous situation but did not feel at ease to delve into this cultural custom.

The capital city of Dakar is a vibrant metropolitan area home to multiple national and regional banks as well as numerous international organizations. We stayed at the Novotel hotel. The influence of French colonization is still very noticeable in restaurants, bakeries, and nightlife. The city is home to as many as 20,000 French expatriates. France still maintains an air force base, and the French fleet is serviced in Dakar's port.

NIGER

The HIV/AIDS project in Niger was also a "problem project," with slow implementation progress. We used Air Senegal to fly from Dakar to Niamey, the capital of Niger, staying at the Grand Hotel du Niger for ten days in August 2007. The Task Team Leder was Djibrilla Karamoko. I conducted many interviews and reviewed earlier reports. The institutional bottleneck was paramount and impeded project performance. The project structure and the institutional arrangements were dysfunctional, the project had not performed well in the past, and would not perform well in the future unless some drastic actions were taken.

The institutional problem of the national HIV/AIDS project had been analyzed in eight separate evaluations between August 2005 and July 2006 by the World Bank, UN agencies (UNAIDS and WHO), donors (GTZ), and by private-sector consulting firms.

All evaluations correctly diagnosed the problem but failed to make a specific recommendation to solve it. Reporting relationships went to two institutional levels: the office of the president and the office of the prime minister. This was the source of the institutional bottleneck and was designed into the project. I made a number of recommendations to remove this obstacle. Key among them was replacing the manager of the Project Coordinating Unit, not for lack of technical competence but for lack of management skills and unwillingness to cooperate with other government entities, especially with the Ministry of Health. The World Bank director in Niger resisted my recommendation to fire a Niger national, but he was let go by the country's president and afterward project performance improved greatly.

Niger is a Francophone Muslim country and a former French colony. It is one of the poorest countries in the world, with minimal government services, and is ranked last in the world on the United Nations Development Index. It also has the world's highest fertility rate (a marriage age of fourteen years being part of the high fertility issue). Niamey lies on the Niger River, and I did not make any field visits outside the capital. I was surprised but appreciative when hearing Bob Marley reggae songs while visiting a covered Sunday market.

Study Tour in Germany and France for a Russian Medical Delegation

This consultancy figures as the most exciting, educational, and enjoyable assignment of my consulting career after my WB retirement. The World Bank received a request from the Russian Federation to organize a study tour for health officials of the Khanty-Mansi Autonomous Okrug (a province in Russia). The objectives of the tour were to study medical and nursing education in Germany and France and to use the findings to improve education in the okrug. The okrug occupies the central part of the West Siberian Plain. The majority (51 percent) of the oil produced in Russia comes from Khanty–Mansi Autonomous Okrug, giving the region great economic importance. With a population of only 1.5 million, the area is sparsely populated. The World Bank would organize and conduct the study tour, but all expenses would be reimbursed by the okrug. To that end, an agreement for advisory services was signed on February 14, 2008, between the okrug and the World Bank, and the cost of services to be provided by the World Bank was set at US$196,705.

I was charged with planning, organizing, and leading the study tour that took place from September 2 to 13, 2008. The participants were five physicians with medical management experience, educational authority, and responsibilities in the okrug, and one Russian staff member of the World Bank office in Moscow. Organization of the German portion of the study tour was contracted out to a German firm specializing in educational tours. We could not find an equivalent firm in France, and it fell upon me to organize the French part of the tour. I corresponded by email with the institutions we wanted to visit in France. My academic appointment at Georgetown University was extremely helpful, as it enabled me to communicate with my French counterparts as a professor, addressing them in my emails as "*Cher collègue.*" For each country we hired two interpreters.

Berlin was the focus of the visits in Germany and included the following activities:

- Lectures at the German Social Insurance Institute presenting the structure and organization of the mandatory health insurance.
- Presentations at the Ministry of Health and Social Affairs on the structure, organization, and management of the German health system.
- A visit to the Trauma Hospital (*Unfallkrankenhaus*), a highly specialized hospital that opened in September 1997 with 538 beds and twenty clinical departments.

- A full day at the Charité Academic Health Center, which integrates a medical school with a university hospital. Its current size of 3,200 beds on four campuses makes it the largest medical school in Europe and the second largest employer in Berlin.
- A visit to the Charité Health Academy, a continuing education center, and its school of nursing.
- A visit to the State Examination Office for Medicine responsible for licensing physicians and allied health professionals and for accrediting faculty and health facilities.
- A visit to the German Medical Association, founded in 1947 and representing the seventeen State Chambers of Physicians. It is mandatory for physicians to be a member of a State Chamber.

Saturday was a free day in Berlin. I had never visited the city and bought a hop-on, hop-off bus and tram ticket to hit all the traditional tourist spots, such as the Brandenburg Gate area, where I had lunch; the Holocaust Memorial, with its 2,711 concrete slabs that form a vast mazelike memorial; the iconic Checkpoint Charlie; and the glass dome of the Reichstag. It was a sunny day, and I walked, looked, and observed to my heart's content.

On Sunday we traveled to Paris, arriving at Charles de Gaulle Airport, where we met the two interpreters and then traveled by minibus to Rennes. I was responsible for all expenditures incurred, and I was surprised at the high cost of driving on French highways when I paid fifty euros for use of the road from Paris to Rennes.

Monday was a full day at the French School of Public Health. France has only one school of public health that serves the whole country. The school admits about 500 graduate students per year and has an average of 1,100 full-time students on campus. An additional 6,000 students are enrolled in professional development and continuing education courses. The 326 permanent faculty members are augmented by 1,600 lecturers and tutors. Master's degrees are offered in French and in English.

After coffee and introductions, we attended a series of five lectures followed by discussions, then had a five-course lunch in the school's private dining room between noon and 2:30 p.m. I missed most of the lunch because the director of the school had asked me to present a lecture to the faculty at 1:00 p.m. At 5:00 p.m., we returned to the hotel. The Russians hired a taxi to visit Mont-Saint-Michel.

The next morning, we were hosted by the School of Medicine of the University of Rennes, which has 3,483 students, 237 faculty members, 50 adjunct faculty members, and 13 research teams collaborating with universities overseas. It has a negotiated and signed agreement with the academic hospital. Professors are civil servants paid by the Ministry of Education, and the hospital pays them a supplement for patient care activities. The dean of the medical school explained the organization and structure of medical education in Rennes. A copious lunch was served, and the Russian delegation very much enjoyed the quality of the French wines. Stories were shared and interpreters were kept busy translating jokes and the lively conversation. We then drove back to the Sofitel Paris Baltimore hotel, and the minibus was a good place to take a siesta en route.

On Wednesday morning we met with the national training advisor for nursing and paramedical professionals at the Ministry of Health's Department of Hospitals and Healthcare, to learn about the status of nursing education in France. A major educational change discussed was requiring nurses to obtain an academic degree instead of a professional one. This issue was also discussed in Germany.

Thursday afternoon we drove to the medical school of the University of Paris 13 (Faculté de médecine). This school of medicine was established in 1970 in a northern industrial suburb of Paris that was economically depressed and socially disadvantaged. The school was created as an "experimental school," testing and carrying out a large number of educational experiments. The empty industrial buildings were converted into an academic environment surrounded by a neighborhood of highly diverse and low income population groups living at the fringes of society. University of Paris 13 is known for its creativity and adaptability to its diverse environment, breaking with traditions and forging a new academic pathway. The dean of the medical school welcomed us and presented the historical perspective of the teaching innovations at the school followed by a visit to the classrooms, the learning laboratories, and the library. A wrap-up meeting at the end of the afternoon featured a synthesis, a general discussion, and a question/answer session. We ended with a champagne toast celebrating the France-Russia friendship.

Friday was the last day of this fascinating study tour, and we all met for a wrap-up meeting at the World Bank office in Paris. A lively discussion ensued on what we had learned, what we could conclude from our visits, and what the next steps would be. From my copious notes I had prepared an outline that guided the discussion. Upon returning to the office, I used the structure of my outline to turn it into a formal thirty-one-page report. I drew a comparison between the two countries, highlighting the duration of studies, the number of students trained annually, the definition and use of admission criteria, the organization of the learning process, the proportion of theory versus practice, the teaching methods, continuing medical education, the use of distance learning, the authority to grant diplomas, the management of medical and nursing schools, and the tenuous agreements between medical schools and university hospitals. The final session deduced implications for the Khanty-Mansi Autonomous Okrug, raising the question of how much and what aspects of the German and French experiences could be applied to their medical and nursing education system.

Some notable observations:

- The study tour had the same objectives and the same participants in both countries and objectives were met in each instance. The major difference I noticed was a greater degree of hospitality in France. Two lunches in Germany were in a hospital cafeteria, and one cold lunch was served at the Ministry of Health and Social Affairs. In France lunches were served in dining rooms as multicourse meals with paired wine, and on the last day, the medical school in Paris toasted the Russian delegation with champagne.
- There is a strong movement in both countries to "professionalize" nursing and require an academic degree instead of a professional one. A nursing degree requires three years of study in both countries. In Germany students can start at the age of sixteen, but in France the minimum starting age for nursing studies is eighteen.
- All students who graduate from high school have equal opportunity to study medicine in France, but Germany requires an entrance examination, and limits the number of students admitted to medical school (numerus clausus).
- Teaching methods have become less focused on classroom lectures and are more problem oriented, competency based, and include hands-on learning. Teaching and learning are intertwined.
- In both countries it takes nine years after secondary education to become a physician.

Reviewing the Ratings of the Implementation Status of Africa Health Projects

The implementation progress of World Bank–financed health projects is measured twice a year using a five-point rating scale. Management of the Africa Region (Director Eva Jarawan) had become concerned about rating inflation and wanted to check the validity of ratings through an independent review. In May 2011, I was invited to be the independent reviewer. I randomly selected six sub-Saharan health projects. All documentation on these projects was made available and I communicated extensively with the task managers responsible for supervising the implementation of these six projects. My report to management showed a downgrading of the assigned ratings in four of the six projects and agreement with the assigned ratings for two projects.

The report included a set of recommendations to improve quality. The common denominator for all six projects was a need for closer management attention at the sector and country levels and recommendations for providing support to the project teams, adjusting the skills mix of the task teams, and more intensive monitoring and more frequent field visits by task teams. Also included were specific quality-improvement suggestions for each of the six projects reviewed.

GUATEMALA

The World Bank contracted me in October 2013 to join a team led by Christine Lao Peña that was tasked with carrying out a functional review of the health sector. I had never visited Guatemala, so I gratefully accepted the offer. We spent one week in Guatemala City collecting data and working with government officials and private-sector institutions while staying at the InterContinental Hotel. Tasks assigned to me included an analysis of the structure and governance of the health-services sector, the supply and demand of the health workforce (availability, distribution, productivity), the procurement and use of pharmaceuticals, and the use of information technology as a management tool. I submitted my twenty-nine-page detailed report with relevant recommendations to the task team leader in December, who incorporated it into the final functional review report along with the contributions from other team members.

About 40 percent of the population (seventeen million) is indigenous. Demographically, Guatemala is one of the youngest countries in the Western Hemisphere, with half of the population being less than twenty years old. It has the worst health outcomes in Latin America, with the highest infant mortality rates and one of the lowest life expectancies at birth in the region. It is one of the poorest countries in Latin America.

The frequent turnover of cabinet ministers for political reasons disrupts long-term plans to strengthen the health sector. A change of minister cascades into replacing vice ministers, directors, and in the case of the health sector, even changing the director of the major hospitals. A hospital director may then change personnel, but the minister of health must approve and sign the changes. This highly centralized decision-making process is a serious weakness in managing effectively and efficiently the most expensive service delivery level of the health system. The heads of clinical departments, on the other hand, are appointed through a competitive process and provide much needed continuity on a day-to-day basis at the clinical operating level. The directors of the two largest hospitals (Roosevelt, with 926 beds, and San Juan de Dios, with 916 beds) were quite ignorant about the operation of the hospital for which they had been officially appointed. Chiefs of clinical departments, on the other hand, were reliable sources of data and information.

COMOROS ISLANDS

In 2001, I had written a health-sector analysis of the Dominican Republic at the request of a World Bank task manager and economist (Philippe Auffret). Twelve years later, in 2013, he still remembered the quality and timeliness of my work and called me, asking me to produce a similarly quality product on the Comoros Islands. Honestly, I must admit that I did not know where these islands were located and had to look it up. Their location in the Indian Ocean east of the Africa coast and close to Madagascar intrigued me, and I accepted the offer.

The Comoros were part of the French colonial empire before becoming independent in 1975. The country (officially the Union of the Comoros) consists of three islands (with French names in parenthesis): Ngazidja (Grande Comore), Mwali (Mohéli), and Nzwani (Anjouan). The capital and largest city, Moroni, is located on Ngazidja. A fourth island, Mayotte, voted against independence from France in 1974 and continues to be administered by France as an overseas department.

Comoros is one of the smallest and poorest countries in the world. Since independence from France, the country experienced more than twenty coups or attempted coups with various heads of state assassinated. Following elections in late 2010, agreement was reached to rotate the presidency among the three islands, inaugurating a period of political stability. Sunni Islam is the dominant religion, practiced by as much as 99 percent of the population. Traditional Comorian women wear colorful sari-like dresses. With fewer than a million people, the Comoros is one of the smallest countries in the world but is one of the most densely populated. The most common language is Comorian, but Arabic and French are also official languages. I worked almost exclusively in French, which is the administrative language and the language used at all formal education levels.

Prosperous Mayotte is the major destination for Comorian

illegal migrants who flee their country. Between 200,000 and 350,000 Comorians live in France and move freely between Mayotte and France.

I flew to Nairobi on KLM on Friday, March 15, 2013, arriving late Saturday, and caught an early flight to Comoros on Monday, March 18, on Kenya Airways—its motto is "The Pride of Africa"—with a stop in Mayotte. Sunday in Nairobi was a rest day, and I played tourist, viewing the city from a hill, feeding the giraffes, and swimming in the hotel pool.

My tasks during my ten day stay included collecting available health-related information, analyzing the health status of the population, assessing whether the provision of health by the public sector, the private sector, and NGOs adequately covered the health needs of the population, and making recommendations to improve population health. My analysis became part of a larger report of social policies (education, health, and social protection) intended to guide the World Bank's support and potential financing interventions.

I stayed at the Sandra Beach Resort on Grande Comore, or Ngazidja, and visited Anjouan Island with an overnight stay, but time did not permit me to visit the third island of Mohéli. Travel among the three islands is by small propeller planes. The hotel on Grand Comore was located on the Indian Ocean, and I excitedly swam for the first time in this ocean to add to my experience swimming in the Atlantic and Pacific Oceans. The French cuisine was locally adapted, the wine came from Lebanon, and the beer from France (Kronenbourg 1664, the best one). I fondly recall sipping a beer on the terrace in the early evening, looking out on the ocean and the lights of the island, and hearing the muezzin call to evening prayer.

Internet connections were available but unreliable, but one anecdote shows how technology makes the world very small. My friend William Hsiao at Harvard's School of Public Health had made a presentation at the World Bank a few months earlier at a memorial for the health economist Philip Musgrove. I needed information on one of his slides for use in my recommendations, so I sent him an email telling him that I was far away somewhere in the Indian Ocean and asked for a copy of his presentation. Unbelievable, but twenty minutes later, I received an email from Bill saying, "Willy, you have no idea where I am. I am in a small village in China for my research project, and attached is my presentation." So much for geographic distances now!

The Millennium Development Goals by 2015

The global health community had agreed on a set of goals to be reached by 2015 to improve population health in developing countries. Of particular concern were Millennium Development Goals (MDG) 4 and 5. MDG 4 called for reducing the under-five mortality rate by two-thirds between 1990 and 2015, and MDG 5 aimed at reducing the maternal mortality ratio per 100,000 live births by three-quarters during the same period. In 2013 progress was insufficient, with a risk of missing the targets.

At a December 2013 meeting of the heads of international development and financing institutions, it was decided to explore options to improve coordinated financing of programs to accelerate progress toward meeting MDGs 4 and 5. Netsanet Workie of the World Bank contracted me for twenty days to prepare an evidence-based report on options, aimed primarily at the heads of agencies and other policymakers at the ministerial level. A draft report, of no more than five thousand words plus references, due by February 12, 2014, was reviewed by World Bank staff and external reviewers. I participated in the review meeting convened by the World Bank and finalized the report by March 12, 2014, together with a PowerPoint version of the report of not more than twenty-five slides.

Options to accelerate progress put forward included financing to accelerate vaccination campaigns to reduce child deaths and financing malaria campaigns; increasing trust funds as an important source of financing; supporting community insurance schemes to mobilize more domestic resources and to expand community-based approaches, and approving financing for MDGs 4 and 5 post-2015 to improve measurement and data collection, rigorous monitoring systems, and evaluating the impact of policies.

The World Bank's Independent Evaluation Group (IEG)

IEG is independent of the management of the World Bank Group (WBG) and reports directly to the executive board. It evaluates the development effectiveness of the World Bank Group. In December 2016 I was invited to join a team led by Antonio Giuffrida to evaluate the World Bank Group Support to Health Services, including all projects and programs approved between July 1, 2005, and June 30, 2016. The purpose of this evaluation was to collect evidence, develop lessons, and propose recommendations that could enhance WBG support to client countries as they move toward universal health coverage (UHC). Team members were assigned to one of four themes: conditional cash transfers; performance-based financing; public-private interactions that integrate private provision of health services with public financing; and pandemics, which are viral outbreaks transmitting readily and spreading fast around the world.

I was assigned to document and analyze the pandemics theme. My focus was on the five main pandemics that occurred during the study period from 2005 to 2016 and on evaluating the World Bank reaction and support to combat these pandemics. The five pandemics subject to my in-depth analysis were:

- The avian influenza, also known as bird flu, which is still active in twenty-six countries.
- The 2009 flu pandemic caused by the H1N1 virus, also known as swine flu, which ended in August 2010. The

U.S. recorded between forty-three million and eighty-nine million cases of H1N1.

- The Middle East respiratory syndrome coronavirus (MERS), a viral respiratory disease first identified in Saudi Arabia in 2012 with cases reported by twenty-seven countries.
- The devastating Ebola crisis in the West African countries of Liberia, Guinea, and Sierra Leone. A total of 28,616 Ebola cases were reported in these three countries, with 11,310 deaths, or a high case-fatality rate of 40 percent. WHO declared the end of the viral outbreak in the three countries in 2016. However, new outbreaks have been reported in 2018 in the Democratic Republic of Congo and are spilling over to Uganda.
- The Zika virus that emerged in Brazil in 2015. WHO declared the end of the outbreak in November 2016. However, a 2018 research study reported that the Zika virus is present in more than eighty-four countries, that the transmission is ongoing, and the virus can be expected to spread.

The 2009 flu pandemic was the only one of the five pandemics that was no longer active in 2017. However, it has become active again, and in 2019 millions of pigs were culled in China and Vietnam. My final report—after several iterations—was submitted and approved on June 16, 2017.

This was my last consultancy. Subsequently, in 2018, I summarized and published my findings in a professional journal: "Evolution of the World Bank Response to Infectious Disease Outbreaks: From a Reactive to a Proactive Approach" (2018), *Journal of Family Medicine and Disease Prevention*, Vol. 4, Issue 2.

MALAWI

The Deutsche Gesellschaft für Internationale Zusammenarbeit (German Corporation for International Cooperation), or GIZ, is a German development agency headquartered in Bonn and Eschborn that provides services in the field of international development cooperation. GIZ mainly implements technical cooperation projects of Germany's Federal Ministry for Economic Cooperation and Development, but it also works with the private sector and other government organizations. It operates ninety offices around the world and considers capacity development to be its core competence.

The Republic of Malawi is a landlocked country in southeast Africa, formerly known as Nyasaland, bordered by Zambia, Tanzania, and Mozambique with an estimated population of 18 million. Its capital is Lilongwe, which is Malawi's largest city. Malawi is Africa's poorest country, with the lowest GDP per capita. Per capita income in 2015 was $350. HIV/AIDS, tuberculosis, and malnutrition accounted for two-thirds of the burden of disease. HIV prevalence is one of the highest in the world, with 10 percent (1.1 million) of the population living with HIV. Corruption within the government is seen as a major obstacle. Homosexuality is illegal. Malawi is a majority Christian country with a large Muslim minority. Infant mortality rates are high, and life expectancy at birth is fifty years. Abortion is illegal except to save the mother's life.

I was contracted by GIZ to study the hospital autonomy component of a development project. The Malawi Ministry of Health wanted to increase the performance of its four central hospitals and asked GIZ for technical assistance to implement its hospital autonomy policy. My earlier experience on hospital autonomy in the Dominican Republic, Lebanon, and Pakistan, as well as my hospital management experience in Mexico and my publications served me well in defining the issues and making relevant recommendations. I visited the central hospital of Lilongwe, asked questions of the director and the staff, interviewed at length the director of the medical stores (which had been granted autonomy four years earlier), and conducted many interviews with government officials. I gained additional information from meetings with NGOs working in the country and from the local staff of the British Department for International Development.

With 70 percent of the health budget coming from international donors, a severe shortage of health workers, and regular stock-outs of medical supplies and pharmaceuticals, it was obvious early on that making the central hospitals autonomous was not the solution to correct the many systemic problems. My budget included seventeen days in the country, and I could have diagnosed the issues and made recommendations in one week.

The consultancy had been scheduled for February 2016 and was subsequently postponed to September. This overlapped with my academic schedule. I was not teaching during the spring semester at Georgetown University, so the earlier February date had been a good fit. The delay conflicted with teaching two courses in the fall semester. Two colleagues kindly agreed to take over three weekly sessions in September: Eva Jarawan on Wednesdays for my undergraduate course, and Nuria Homedes on Tuesdays for my graduate course.

The Salima district, bordering Lake Malawi (which takes up about a third of the country), and the beach at Senga Bay is the weekend retreat of the upper class from the capital. On a Sunday three of us hired a car and driver to go to the beach, where we walked along the water, saw a burkini* for the first time, ate fresh fish for lunch, and returned in a hot car driving on deteriorating roads. My two companions were a Norwegian professor who specialized in data collection for monitoring progress and a Spanish lady from Bilbao living in Germany who spoke German fluently,

*A burkini is a type of modesty swimsuit for women. The suit covers the whole body except the face, hands, and feet and is light enough for swimming. The design is intended to respect Islamic traditions of modest dress.

having attended the German School in Bilbao. The four German colleagues preferred to stay at the hotel to work and relax. Incidentally, of the four Germans, three were cigarette smokers. Quite ironic when working on a health project. I had never before been on a health mission with a team member who smoked.

My flight there, on Friday, September 2, was a twelve-hour nonstop flight to Addis Ababa on Ethiopian Airlines, connecting Saturday morning to Lilongwe. The longer flight time allows more hours of sleep than a shorter eight-hour flights, reducing somewhat the effects of jetlag. The return flight on Tuesday afternoon, September 20, followed the same itinerary, changing planes in Addis Ababa, and leaving in the evening to arrive the next morning at 8:10 a.m. at Dulles International Airport. The Ethiopian Airlines business-class club in Addis is the best club I had ever spent time waiting in throughout my entire flying experience. The return flight, however, made a refueling stop in Shannon, Ireland, because the easterly winds add flying time. This meant that we were woken for landing in Shannon around 5:00 a.m. before crossing the Atlantic.

It was on this trip that I learned about the persecution of people with albinism, which is based on the belief that certain body parts of albinos can transmit magical powers. This superstition is prevalent in some parts of the African Great Lakes region, where witch doctors and others use body parts as ingredients in rituals, concoctions, and potions with the claim that their magic will bring prosperity to the user. As a result, people with albinism have been persecuted, killed, and dismembered, and graves of albinos have been dug up and desecrated. Conversely, people with albinism have been ostracized and even killed because they are presumed to be cursed and bring bad luck. Albinism is a genetically inherited condition and is very rare, affecting about one in 20,000 people worldwide. While it's rare in the Western world, it's quite common in sub-Saharan Africa, likely as a result of consanguinity.

This was my last international consultancy and happened to

be the easiest. It was a good way of retiring from flying and working internationally. The Malawi experience motivated me to write and publish an article in a peer-reviewed professional journal: "Does Autonomy for Public Hospitals in Developing Countries Increase Performance? Evidence-Based Case Studies" (*Social Science & Medicine*, Volume 179, April 2017, pages 74–80).

6 PROFESSIONAL PRESENTATIONS AND INTERNATIONAL SYMPOSIA: 1997–2018

UZBEKISTAN

The American International Health Alliance, established in 1992, supports international collaboration and technical assistance. On April 20 to 24, 1997, it organized a conference on Healthcare Workforce for the Twenty-First Century in Tashkent, Uzbekistan. My colleague Gary Filerman suggested my name as a conference participant. My lecture presented a "Conceptual Framework for Discussing Health Workforce Development," and my slides were shown on two screens: on the left in English and on the right in Russian. I remember leaving Tashkent on a 3:45 a.m. flight to Frankfurt.

GERMANY

Heidelberg University is a public research university founded in 1386 and Germany's oldest university. The Institute of Tropical Hygiene and Public Health (now the Institute of Public Health) offers a Master of Science in International Health. The institute director, Dr. Rainer Sauerborn, invited me in February 1998 to meet with the faculty to discuss global health issues and funding sources and for presenting a graduate class lecture. A shuttle takes passengers from Frankfurt Airport to the city of Heidelberg.

MEXICO

In November 1997 I attended a conference in Mexico City and presented a paper on quality assurance at the invitation of the Comisión Nacional de Arbitraje Médico (National Medical Arbitration Commission).

ECUADOR

The Latin American Faculty of Social Sciences, or Facultad Latino Americana de Ciencias Sociales (FLACSO), supports the creation of social science institutions to help the development of Latin American societies. It was created in 1957 and incorporates seventeen Latin American and Caribbean countries.

The Ecuador chapter invited me as a visiting professor in April 2003 to teach a course on the Economy and Organization of Health Systems with an emphasis on a comparative analysis of the health systems of thirteen countries (Ecuador, Colombia, Costa Rica, Chile, Mexico, Bolivia, Canada, U.S., Peru, Venezuela, Argentina, Cuba, Dominican Republic). The sessions for the two-week course ran from 7:00 to 10:00 a.m., as almost all students were physicians employed full time. In the afternoon I met with other faculty members to provide technical assistance. Some Ecuadorean physicians had worked in Colombia and recounted the very different organizational structures there, having to stay within agreed-on budgets and apply strict cost controls. The Ecuadorean currency had been dollarized—it had previously been the sucre—and my expenses and honoraria were paid in dollars. However, the $20 bill was the largest currency bill available at all banks, and I ended up with a wad of dollar bills.

For the second invitation by FLASCO, in 2005, I participated in a virtual course on Policies and Management of Health organized for health professionals of the South American societies of the International Federation of Red Cross and Red Crescent Societies in cooperation with WHO/PAHO. The course consisted of one session per week from April 25 to June 17, 2005. This was a new but utterly frustrating experience. I would sit at home in front of my computer, and I could hear the participants, who were based in many South American countries, greeting each other upon arrival. Questions and answers appeared as texts on my screen in a chat format. While typing an answer to one question, another question would pop up on the screen not related to the question I was responding to. Students would at times insert their written opinion, and it was impossible to follow a logical trend of thought. Technologies nowadays are able to manage a virtual approach using Skype or Zoom, showing texts or slides on the screen, raising hands to request a turn to speak, etc. All this did not exist in 2005 and I ended this academic experience quite dissatisfied.

THE RUSSIAN FEDERATION

At the request of the Russian Government, the World Bank organized a two-week course in September 2006 on Health Sector Reform and Sustainable Financing in the Chuvash Republic, a unit of the Russian Federation. Two U.S. colleagues and I conducted the workshop: George Schieber on financing and provider payment, Rifat Atun on quality of service delivery, and myself on health systems. Lectures were also presented by Russian colleagues. The course was attended by forty-one participants from the Chuvash Republic, the Voronezh Oblast, the Chechen Republic, and the Republic of Armenia. The venue was a large building in the midst of a pine forest on the Volga River—it was used as a rest and recuperation area that was part of the Russian health system, a leftover of the Soviet era, when workers were allowed to go to a "spa" for health reasons.

The faculty was housed in the VIP section of the building and the assigned rooms were small suites: a bedroom, bathroom, and a very small sitting area with a TV that only broadcasted Russian programs. Downstairs was a computer room with internet access that was only open from 9:00 a.m. to 5:00 p.m., when we were mostly in the classroom next door. Our request for access in the evening hours was declined.

This was my first experience teaching with simultaneous translation by two interpreters. We made our lectures and PowerPoint presentations available to the interpreters to ensure their understanding of the subject matter and of the technical terms. I am sure that they did a competent job. However, there is a time lag between what the speaker says and when the students hear it. This was frustrating, as I was used to reading the audience's facial expressions to get instant feedback on their interest and understanding, or their agreeing or disagreeing. In this case, I was already on the next point when the students heard and were reacting to the previous one.

Paying for our room and the meals presented us with a problem, as the "spa" only accepted local currency and no credit cards. Dollars could be exchanged at a commercial bank in the capital city, Cheboksary, forty-five minutes away. I did not carry sufficient dollars, but George did, and I borrowed $300 from him. A Russian colleague went to Cheboksary to change the dollars and we paid our bills in rubles. This was one of my most memorable teaching experiences, but I never did teach again using simultaneous translation.

7 ACADEMIC APPOINTMENTS: 1997–2018

Upon retiring from the World Bank, I became academically active, first with the George Washington University (GW). Professor Richard Riegelman was the founding dean of the School of Public Health—later renamed the Milken Institute School of Public Health—and when he returned to his previous position of professor of epidemiology and biostatistics, Professor Richard Southby, who was associate dean, became acting dean. I had worked with Dr. Southby before my retirement from the World Bank, partly as a guest lecturer and as a member of a team creating a distance-learning course.

GW appointed me in 1997 to the academic staff as adjunct professor of Health Services Management and Policy for the academic year 1997–1998 and renewed the appointment each year for the next four years.

The School of Nursing and Health Studies (SNH) at Georgetown University (GU) considered creating a Department of International Health in 2002. My friend Gary Filerman was on the SNH faculty as chair of the Department of Health Systems Administration and had proposed it. He consulted with me on who would be a good fit to lead the new department. I recommended Dr. Bernhard Liese, who was about to retire from the World Bank, and Bernhard was appointed as chair of the Department of International Health. I had worked with Bernhard on numerous World Bank health projects, and he invited me to join him as an adjunct professor. I signed my first GU contract on September 3, 2004, for the academic year 2004–2005.

My first teaching assignment at GU was to conduct a weekly seminar in the fall semester of 2004 for international postdoctoral students sponsored by USAID's International East Central European Health Leadership Training Program. This twelve-month program of U.S.-based training was designed for East European participants who could become leaders in organizing, managing, financing, and evaluating health services and in developing health policy options. Students—many medical doctors—came from Romania, Bulgaria, and Macedonia. I structured and taught a doctoral seminar called Equity and Quality Dimensions of Health Systems. Field visits were organized to the Washington, D.C., VA Medical Center with special attention to its electronic medical records system VISTA; the Holy Cross Hospital in Silver Spring, Maryland; the Inova Hospital in Arlington, Virginia; and of course, the MedStar Georgetown University Hospital.

A Comparative Health Systems course was added to the Department of International Health undergraduate program, which I taught for nine years, from the spring semester of 2008 until the fall semester of 2016. Average class size was about thirty students, mostly female and mostly white. I co-taught the course one more year in the fall semester of 2017 with my colleague Eva Jarawan before handing the course over to her in 2018.

The Department of International Health initiated a master's program in Global Health in 2013, for which I structured the course Health Policy and Systems, teaching it for five years, until 2017. The last year I team-taught the course with Eva Jarawan, and she took over in 2018. Graduate students typically have a job, and courses are offered in the evening. This meant that for four years I taught graduate students on Tuesdays from 5:00 to 7:30 p.m. and undergraduates on Wednesdays from 12:30 to 3:00 p.m. Driving eighty-five miles home on Tuesday evenings at 8:00 p.m. and then returning to GU the next morning at the age of eighty-one was stressful and tiring. I would stay overnight at a motel in Arlington, Virginia the first year. The next year the department made reservations at a nearby hotel. When my son Lieven married in June 2015 and bought a house in Washington, D.C., I stayed overnight in his guest room. A lower energy level and a slight hearing loss at the age of eighty-six became irreversible obstacles to continue this schedule, so I stopped teaching in 2018 and continued as a faculty member for the academic year 2018–2019 to assist in reviewing student papers and for grading exercises.

Three additional academic responsibilities in other schools of GU are noteworthy. The Department of Government at Georgetown University had an agreement with the University of Salzburg Business School to host a group of students each year for a ten-day immersion into U.S. government policy issues. These students were enrolled at the Salzburg University in the International Executive MBA Public & Health Care Management program. The students were public-sector managers. The program included a half-day seminar on health care for the subgroup of health care managers. Between 2013 to 2018, I taught this seminar, which I enjoyed very much because, for one, a small group seminar setting lends itself to lively discussions and fruitful interactions and, two, these "students" were mid-career professionals with practical experience that leads to challenging questions.

Guest lectures in other GU schools included a lecture on health systems for first-year medical students—purportedly to widen their horizon, but students were not interested—and a lecture on global health systems to fourth-year medical students and residents in family medicine who were interested and asked many questions.

GU's McCourt School of Public Policy offers a master's degree in public policy, and I worked with student teams in the Comparative Public Management course who had selected studying a global health issue. I was also on a committee to interview and recommend students for a potential Fulbright scholarship.

A cardiac arrest, followed by triple bypass surgery, in January 2017 and a right carotid artery surgery (endarterectomy) in February 2018 were clear messages to slow down and prepare for real retirement. The 2019–2020 academic year started without me, and I truly missed it!

8 REFLECTIONS

Rereading the long account of my professional career, I am left with concrete facts but also with unanswered questions. Have I been successful? In what? And how do you define success? Financial and professional success can be measured and documented objectively. Financial results are measured as net worth in liquid assets and property. Professional success is shown by earning academic degrees (B.A., M.S., Ph.D.), academic appointments at prestigious universities (University of Minnesota, George Washington University, Georgetown University), promotions at the World Bank, multiple publications in peer-reviewed scientific journals, and sustained demand for my consultancy services by international multilateral and bilateral organizations.

Yet success does not negate feelings of insecurity. Did I do well because I knew the rules of the game and learned quickly how to play the game? Was I a fraud? I recall buying and reading a 1985 book by Joan Harvey on being a fraud (*If I'm So Successful, Why Do I Feel Like a Fake?*). Working with colleagues whom I saw as more intelligent, more creative, better public speakers and presenters, and having quicker minds fed my insecurities.

Then why was I invited to join teams, be given more responsibility, and be promoted? Jumbled and contradictory feelings often crowded my mind.

My modest family beginnings in Belgium would not have predicted my academic and global health accomplishments. The fourth-grade education of my mother and the eighth-grade education of my father stand in sharp contrast with the education of the parents of colleagues at the World Bank. Their parents were typically university-educated lawyers, physicians, economists, etc. It was self-evident for their children to follow in their footsteps. In my case, the stunning leap in the level of education in a single generation deserves noting.

Where have I failed? Did I travel too much? Why did I? What motivated me? Professionalism? Being on the road? Curiosity? Learning about countries from the inside and not being a tourist? Inborn sense of adventure? Desire to learn? All of the above? Did some factors exert a stronger pull than others? Is it possible to weigh the contribution of each factor?

Why was my career worthwhile and meaningful? What survived in me from the rigid Roman Catholic upbringing was a deep conviction that as human beings we should "love your neighbor like yourself" (Leviticus 19:18) and that we are accountable to make the world a better place for all. Am I my brother's keeper? Yes, I am. The idea of service permeates my whole career. First, as a teacher in Belgium helping teenage students learn. Second, teaching health professionals in Latin America to improve their management skills. Third, at the World Bank, designing, supervising, and assessing health projects aimed at reducing the burden of disease and improving the health conditions of people in less developed countries. Fourth, sharing my global health experiences by teaching undergraduate and graduate students, conducting research, and publishing.

Looking back, I feel blessed and grateful. I feel proud of my achievements and thankful to the people who believed in me, supported me, and provided me with opportunities to serve. Ultimately, a major source of pride is that what I have, and what I leave behind, I earned myself through hard work and dogged perseverance. My achievements overshadow the inevitable human failures.

—W. De Geyndt, December 2023

Made in the USA
Middletown, DE
20 November 2024

64776123R00076